P9-DUC-022

From the Library
of
Blake D. Konzol

Spanish-Colonial
Architecture
in the
United States

Spanish Fountain, Residence of Mr. A. I. Root, Los Angeles, California
Carleton M. Winslow, Architect

Spanish-Colonial Architecture in the United States

REXFORD NEWCOMB

DOVER PUBLICATIONS, INC.
New York

Published in Canada by General Publishing Company, Ltd., 30 Lesmill Road, Don Mills, Toronto, Ontario.
Published in the United Kingdom by Constable and Company, Ltd., 10 Orange Street, London WC2H 7EG.

This Dover edition, first published in 1990, is an unabridged and unaltered republication of the work first published by J.J. Augustin, New York, in 1937.

Manufactured in the United States of America
Dover Publications, Inc., 31 East 2nd Street, Mineola, N.Y. 11501

Library of Congress Cataloging-in-Publication Data

Newcomb, Rexford, 1886–1968.
  Spanish-colonial architecture in the United States / Rexford Newcomb.
       p.   cm.
    Reprint. Originally published: New York : J.J. Augustin, 1937.
    ISBN 0-486-26263-4
    1. Architecture, Spanish colonial—United States.   I. Title.
  NA707.N44   1990
  720'.973—dc20
                                                                    90-30480
                                                                       CIP

TO THE MEMORY OF MY FATHER
THE LATE
FREDERICK EXELER NEWCOMB (NEUKAMM)
THIS VOLUME IS DEDICATED

Foreword

It is twenty years since the author's "Franciscan Mission Architecture of Alta California" first acquainted readers with the character and details of Spanish-Colonial Architecture in what is now the United States. At that time the California variant of the Spanish Colonial had far greater popular appeal than the sister styles of Arizona, New Mexico, Texas or Florida. Therefore only Spanish-Colonial architecture in the Golden State was featured in that volume.

In the interim, however, these other worthy varieties of the Spanish manner have come to be valued, not only for their intrinsic worth, but also for the wealth of suggestion which they offer for present-day work in the areas in which they are indigenous. Indeed, much excellent modern work has already been accomplished in the spirit of each of these local variants. In view of this fact it has seemed expedient to produce an entirely new work including not only the architecture of Spanish-Colonial California but also historic examples from each of those states where the Spanish Colonial developed a worthy architectural expression. To these have been added examples of modern work that embody successful adaptations of the indigenous historic spirit in each of these states.

The scheme of the volume is simple. It is divided into eight general sections. Of these, the first two treat the historical and artistic backgrounds of the Spanish-Colonial movement; the next five delineate by means of measured drawings, photographs and worded descriptions the characteristics of the fine old structures erected during the Colonial period, and the final section presents the best work of contemporary architects who have drawn upon this historic resource. It is hoped that the historic examples will inspire further modern work and that the contemporary examples will indicate the general versatility of the Spanish Colonial in adapting itself to modern usage.

If the amount of material included in the section on California should seem to outweigh that of other states, this is to be accounted for on the grounds that the wealth of historic examples in California is greater than that of any other state and that California was earlier in recognizing the possibilities of and has been more generally alive to the splendid inspiration which historic precedent offered for modern accomplishment.

The author's thanks are due to the J. B. Lippincott Co. for permission to use some drawings and photographs included in a former work by him. On the numerous plates credit has been given to the various photographers who have so generouslly permitted their works to be reproduced, but the author desires further to acknowledge his deep indebtedness to these gentlemen, particularly to Mr. Atlee B. Ayres, Architect of San Antonio who at the suggestion of the author undertook a photographic record of the Texas missions. His sincere thanks are also due Mr. H. Pascal Webb of Los Ángeles for his photograph of the facade of Mission San Diego de Alcalá, to Mr. J. Marshall Miller, architect for the restoration, for photographs of various details of the restored San Diego de Alcalá, to Harvey Patterson of San Antonio for views of the Texas missions and the old Governor's Palace, to H. L. Summerfield for his view of San Antonio de Valero (Alamo), to Putman and Valentine for many views of the southwest, and to numerous friends who have allowed the use of photographs from their private collections. He would add an expression of his deep appreciation to the various architects who have cooperated by lending plans or photographs of their works. To all these he is under deep obligation.

COLLEGE OF FINE AND APPLIED ARTS
UNIVERSITY OF ILLINOIS
JUNE 1, 1937

Rexford Newcomb

Contents

Plates

[*13*]

I. Historical Note

Of colonial architecture the territory now comprising the United States had two sorts, the English Colonial of the Atlantic Coast and the Spanish Colonial of the Gulf States and Southwest. Volumes have been written concerning our interesting and beautiful English-Colonial architecture but comparatively little has been said of that other, and just as important, architectural expression which grew up in that vast territory, now within the United States, that was once ruled by the proud monarchs of Old Spain.

This territory may be said to have extended from the present Mexican boundary northward including that part of the present California south of Sonoma, all of Arizona and New Mexico, most of Florida and Texas, and portions of the Gulf States. Indeed we should remember that at one time the Spanish domain in what is now the United States was conceived as embracing all that trackless area west of the Mississipi, and that the intrepid Coronado, as early as 1541, penetrated this region to a point nearly as far north as the present southern boundary of Nebraska. However, the geographical extent of actual Spanish occupation is embraced by the American states already named.

Spanish conquest of North America began with the subjugation of Mexico in 1519 at which time the great Aztec chieftain, Montezuma, and his followers were defeated by Cortez. No sooner were Spanish arms victorious in New Spain than the subjugation of the heathen for Christ and the Cross was begun. In fact missionary efforts in the New World date from the Bull of May 3, 1493, when Alexander VI directed their Catholic majesties to send to America "worthy, God-fearing, learned, skilled, and experienced men in order to instruct the inhabitants in the Catholic faith."

Even before Cortez' conquest of Mexico we hear of the arrival in Hispañola of a band of Dominicans (1510). Soon also the Franciscans reached Mexico and by 1535, the records contain the names of over one hundred friars of these orders. The documents of the time, many of which are preserved, indicate the wide part which these friars took in the exploration as well as the Christianization of New Spain.

Up to 1590 the Franciscans and the Dominicans were the principal missionary agents, but during that year the Society of Jesus (Jesuits), founded in 1539, entered the Mexican missionary field. Within ten years this zealous band had not only made a place for itself in the religious endeavors of the New World but had established eight mission churches in northern Mexico, which number was, by 1644, increased to some thirty-five establishments, principally in Sinaloa and Sonora.

In 1681 *Padre* Eusebio Francisco Kino came to Mexico as royal cosmographer. Soon, however, his Jesuitic zeal manifested itself in a desire to take the field as a missionary and he was allowed to take up work in northern Mexico and southern Arizona where he labored among the Pima Indians. It was he who established the Pius Fund of the Californias, a fund which, contributed to by wealthy Spaniards and Mexicans, made possible the support of the mission *padres* who later went to *Baja* California (the peninsula), and to *Alta* California (the present American state). Kino was the actual founder of the missions of *Baja* California, establishing the first church in the peninsula at Loreto in October, 1697. His zeal later carried him to Arizona where he established Mission San Xavier del Bac in May, 1700.

The Jesuits labored diligently in *Baja* California and by 1735 the mission system in this sterile peninsula was upon a firm financial basis. Dissatisfaction with the Jesuits in Mexico and indeed throughout all Spanish domain was gathering, however, and in 1767, the storm broke with the result that all members of this order were expelled from Spanish territory.

It was just at this time that the viceroys of Mexico were interested in the occupation of what is now our American California. Thus, the Jesuit missions in *Baja* California were first turned over to the administration of the Franciscans, who by this time were doing excellent missionary duty in northern Mexico and Texas. The Franciscans took charge of the peninsular churches in July, 1768, but since this order proposed also to take up the Christianization of *Alta* California the crown ordered a division of labors. The result was that the Franciscans were given a free rein in all of California north of San Diego Bay, while the old Jesuit missions of the peninsula to the south were turned over to the Dominicans (April, 1770).

Thus in July, 1769, *Padre* Junípero Serra began the establishment of that chain of mission churches that, until secularization in 1834—35, was to be the backbone of Spanish-Mexican civilization in California and the principal colonizing agency for most of that time. This chain which embraced at first the territory between San Diego and Monterey was extended to San Francisco Bay by 1776, and to Sonoma by 1823.

As a result of Jesuit expulsion, the establishments in Arizona, of which there were several, amongst them San Gabriel de Guevavi (1692), San José de Tumacácori (1697), San Cayetano de Calabasas (1694), Santa Gertrudes de Tubac and San Xavier del Bac (1700), were also transferred to the care of the Franciscans. So fervent was the Franciscan zeal that, by 1776, the friars of that order had in hand a virile missionary movement in what is now Arizona, the chief missionary centres of which were the old Jesuit posts of Guevavi, now renamed Los Santos Ángeles de Guevavi, and San Xavier del Bac. The great church of San Xavier, so much admired, was not erected until 1797 and is thus of Franciscan rather than Jesuitic design.

In addition to these establishments in southern Arizona, which may be considered as the most northernly of a chain reaching up through Sonora, there were early Jesuit missions among the Zuñis of northern Arizona. Nothing of architectural interest attaches to these latter, however, and for our purpose they are negligible.

The Franciscan fathers were in New Mexico very early, establishing a post near San Juan de los Caballeros, thirty-one miles north of Santa Fé, in 1598 or fully one hundred and seventy years before the first establishment in California. No remnant of this early church remains although it was replaced by the mission in the *Pueblo* of San Juan. Other churches were established in rapid succession, an early one at Santa Fé in 1607. This was the old church of San Miguel, still in use, for which the earlier date of 1541, is often claimed. We are told that *Padre* Alonzo de Benavides began a church at Santa Fé in 1626 (this was probably the church of San Francisco now replaced by the cathedral) and that, by the end of the century, the town boasted two others, Our Lady of Guadalupe (1640) and the *Capilla* Rosario (Chapel of the Rosary) (1692). The Church of Our Lady of Light was not erected until 1785.

Many of the mission churches in New Mexico have fallen into ruin but excellent work is being done by public-spirited organizations working for the preservation of these interesting and worthy remainders of Spanish occupation. That New Mexico was under the banner of Old Spain longer (nearly three centuries) than she has been enrolled among the company of American states, should serve to emphasize the importance of preserving for future generation this long and colorful past.

Because of the influence of the primitive structural forms, developed by the *pueblo* (town-dwelling) Indians, long before the appearance of the Spaniards, the Spanish-Colonial architecture of New Mexico was of a very different character from that developed in other states. It may be said to be almost equally Indian and Spanish; Spanish in plan, form and idea; Indian in methods of construction and detail. As a result it has a quaint, barbaric interest not to be matched elsewhere. This original and distinctive local variant, now often called the Santa Fé School, is being utilized to the full in the construction of modern buildings in this unique and interesting capital.

In Texas the Franciscans were also laboring. By 1621 they appear to have established a post on Matagorda Bay, known as Our Lady of Loreto. But Franciscan activity in Texas dates principally from the early eighteenth century, the first third of which saw the establishment of something like a dozen missions, five of which, San Antonio de Valero (Alamo), San José y San Miguel de Aguayo, Nuestra Señora de la Purísima Concepción de Acuña, San Francisco de la Espada, and San Juan de Capistrano were in the vicinity of the present city of San Antonio.

From the facts set forth above it will be seen that the architectural expression connected with the mission movement was almost completely due to Franciscan religious zeal and managerial ability.

The Franciscan scheme of Christianization looked forward to making of the Indian a true child of the Church, a loyal subject of the King of Spain, and a God-fearing, self-respecting and self-supporting citizen. The mission program was administered to bring about these results. Such a program called for the following structures conveniently arranged, readily administrable, and easily defended: a church, a house for the *padres*, shops for the various crafts and trades taught to the Indians, store houses, a kitchen, a dining-room, a guard room for the small military escort, a cemetery, a hospital, quarters for young women, young men, and domestics, barns, corrals and other farm structures, and a village for the Indian families. In some of the desert sections, to be sure, agriculture was not so widely practiced as in California, thus the building program varied somewhat.

As a usual thing the buildings were arranged around a courtyard *(patio)* flanked by arcaded, cloister-like walks which thus afforded communication between the buildings. The church and cemetery were usually at the side of the *patio* and thus a little removed from the busy centre of communal activity.

Two padres were usually appointed to each mission, one in charge of spiritual matters, the other in charge of temporal affairs. They taught the Indians Christian doctrine, the Scriptures, some Spanish, singing (to the more alert) and one or another of the simple crafts or trades such as carpentry, shoe-making, basketry, pottery, stock raising, butchering, fruit growing, and the various branches of agriculture. Often a soldier of the guard could assist in the teaching and in some cases was compensated by the government for his trouble. By a judicious administration of the great landed estates which they preëmpted and a careful husbanding of their resources, often large temporal fortunes were built up by the missions.

The daily routine of course varied somewhat with the different localities, but was about as follows. The day opened with the Angelus at sunrise which called the Indians to assemble in the chapel where they were required to attend morning prayers and mass, and where they received religious instruction. After mass, breakfast was served, following which each went to his work. At eleven o'clock dinner was eaten and this

[20]

was followed by a *siesta* which lasted until 2 P. M. Work was then resumed and continued until an hour before sunset, when the Angelus recalled all to worship in the church. After prayers and rosary, supper was eaten and the time from then on until nine o'clock was devoted to recreation.

The young men and young women lived at the mission proper, the young women being under the care of a trusted Indian matron who was responsible for their welfare and their training in the crafts. The dormitory which they occupied was known as *monjeria* or *convento*. Here the girl lived until she had been wooed and won by an Indian youth and they had indicated their intention of marriage. After marriage the couple settled down in a hut in the Indian village near by. Courtship took place through the barred windows of the *convento* after the fashion of courtships in Mexico and Spain. While temporal activities varied with the districts, many of the missions made substantial progress with agriculture and fruit growing and devised irrigation works, water-supply systems and, in some cases, grist and saw mills.

II. The Spanish Architectural Tradition

The Spanish-Colonial architecture of the Southwest, while it was thoroughly expressive of the pioneer life and setting which gave it birth, was nevertheless the result of a long heredity which influenced it and colored its expression. That heredity is traceable back through Mexico to the mother country, Spain.

But Spanish architecture itself had had a vari-colored heredity. Spain was originally inhabited by the Iberians who were doubtless a division of a great early Mediterranean race. Into Spain eventually came the Romans who, when their power waned, were succeeded by the Visi-goths. In the early eighth century the Visi-goths were conquered by the Moors and the Moors were eventually driven out, after seven hundred years of occupation, as the result of an expansive movement of the successors of these very Visi-goths whom they had driven northward into the Pyrenees in 711.

Thus we may see that Spanish blood, Spanish institutions and consequently Spanish architecture was of necessity cosmopolitan. But the primitive Iberians were not great architects; therefore the real beginnings of architecture in Spain may be said to date from the period of Roman domination. The Moors contributed a certain oriental quality, many effects of which are to be detected in the provincial expressions of Texas, Arizona and California.

Whereas Spanish art after the success of Christian arms was affected by all the vogues that swept western Europe, the impress of the Romanesque and Gothic, as such, is not to be sensed in any large measure in Spanish-Colonial architecture. However that repoussé-like quality of the decoration of the Plateresque period, which indeed was predicated upon the intricacies of Spanish Gothic decoration, was the forerunner of the unrestrained and over decorative Churrigueresque style, that fanciful and unstructural mood of the Renaissance in Spain, the influence of which is most surely felt in much of the architecture of the Spanish colonies. In this sense the influence of the Spanish Gothic was passed on to Mexico and our own Southwest. In Mexico, as in Spain, the flying buttress expressed in classic dress is often seen and indeed in the buttresses of Mission San Xavier de Bac (Arizona) we note a reminiscence of the Gothic of Old Spain as surely as in the pointed arches of Mission San José y San Miguel de Aguayo near San Antonio (Texas) or in the vaulted baptistry of Mission San Carlos Borromeo (Carmel), California.

But we must recall that the early Plateresque of Spain (1500—1556), with its Gothic-Moresque intricacies of detail, was followed by a classic reaction led by Herrera, who exemplified in such structures as the Escorial, his creed of the classic. The belated reflection of this classic reaction which lasted in Spain up to 1650 is to be seen in the sober Doric details of many a Spanish-Colonial church of New Spain, as at the *Capilla Real* (Royal Chapel) Montererey, and Mission Santa Bárbara, California.

The Churrigueresque, that most decorative and unarchitectural of all Renaissance styles — the Baroque of Spain — was in vogue when much of the Spanish-Colonial architecture of Mexico was being erected. However, a second return to classic purity which dominated Spanish architecture during the latter half of the eighteenth century, accounts for the chastened character of many a provincial church in the Spanish colonies.

When the Spaniards arrived in Mexico they began, naturally, to build in the fashion of their home land. Prescott tells us that after the ancient Aztec city of Montezuma had been razed, a new city was built upon the site. The Spaniards appropriated few, if any, of the ancient Aztec forms although, through the employment of native labor, a certain barbaric splendor eventually made itself felt in Mexican architecture. And indeed a measure of this filtered through to the outlying provincial churches of our own Southwest.

The priests, who were in most cases the builders, had not received the necessary professional training to make them good architects and in attempting to raise to the Glory of God houses of worship in the wilderness they fell into many difficulties, difficulties which we should criticize with the utmost charity. The Texan and Arizonan churches, being in lands more or less accessible from Mexico, were built in a style closely resembling the great churches of Mexico where professional architects, some of them sent from Spain, executed the work. In these two Colonial expressions we find the same attempt at magnificance and grandeur, the same over-decorated facades, the same bare walls. The Texan and Arizonan churches have a certain oriental atmosphere due to the use of domes, and a visit to San Xavier del Bac is like a voyage to some enchanged land of the Moslems, so oriental is its architecture. The churches of these states are more elaborate, both in outline and in decoration, than those of either New Mexico or California. But we have to remember that in the case of San José y San Miguel de Aguayo near San Antonio, a sculptor was sent from Mexico to execute the carving.

As it was difficult to attract workmen to California and New Mexico, the *padres* aided by their Indians, with humble materials and unskilled hands, were compelled to build simply. And meeting squarely the problem as they saw it, they were able to create a style, which for the country in which it was developed, has not been excelled. The charm of the New Mexican and Californian churches may in a measure be said to consist of a certain naive simplicity and a rugged straight-forwardness that is as interesting as it is rare.

The Spanish Colonial, coming as it did from Spain through Mexico, like a beam of light reflected through a prism, diverged into the various provincial expressions which we have named. Each locality brought forth, as time progressed, a distinctive style; thus the work in California, New Mexico, Arizona, Texas and Florida differ from each other very materially in character and spirit. Some of these distinctions are extremely difficult to define in words and only a study of the following plates will serve to enforce this truth upon the reader. However, certain salient characteristics of each may be set down in analytical fashion and thus express for the reader the distinguishing divergent features. These will be found adjacent to the particular variant to which they refer.

III. *Spanish-Colonial Architecture in Florida*

The old Spanish city of Saint Augustine founded in 1565 by Pedro Menéndez de Avilés contains the principal remains of Spanish-Colonial architecture in what is now the state of Florida. Spanish missions were built in Florida and in what is now Georgia, but these have so completely disappeared that little regarding their architecture is known. It is Saint Augustine therefore to which we repair for our best knowledge of the Spanish Colonial in Florida. Here the following important examples are to be seen and examined.

Building	*Date*
The Old Cathedral	1791
Castle San Marco (now Fort Marion)	1638—1756
Old Spanish Gate	16th century
Slave Market	

An examination of the salient features of these structures permits the cataloging of the following traits:

Materials of construction : Coquina, a soft whitish stone composed of crushed shells and coral cemented together and found abundantly in this section, was much used. "Tabby" (from the Spanish word *tapia)* a mixture of gravel, shells and oyster-shell lime was also employed. These in addition to *adobe* and stone formed the principal materials for wall construction.

Roofs were framed of wood and during the early times covered with thatch. This thatch was later replaced by tiles.

Architectural Characteristics : Plain, unadorned walls, simple masses, heavy bastions and turrets (especially upon fortifications), classic pediments and orders around openings, moulded windows, curved pierced gables (upon the Cathedral), square detached piers or columns (Slave Market) characterize the style in Florida.

[25]

IV. Spanish-Colonial Architecture in Texas

"When Cabeza de Vaca in 1536 straggled into Culiacan from Florida after an eight year's jaunt through a 'no man's land'," says Hammond,[1] "his stories, retold by hungry fortune seekers, were sufficiently astounding to provide anyone with material for dreams of great conquests in the interior." In the hearts of ambitious soldiers and laymen these stories enkindled visions of vast landed estates and great wealth in gold; in the hearts of the faithful *padres* of Saint Francis they awakened dreams of another sort of conquest—the conquering of the wilderness for Christ and the Church.

Cabeza de Vaca who had traversed large areas in Texas was followed in 1540—42 by Don Francisco Vasquez de Coronado and others who helped to round out Spanish information regarding that trackless area which we now call the State of Texas. But despite the interest of adventurers and clergy, Texas was to remain undisturbed until the 1680's when the threat of French invasion of a territory that was clearly in Spain's path of destiny spurred the Viceroys in Mexico into action. Following the establishment of two missions by the Spanish near El Paso, the French under the Sieur de la Salle started a colony on Matagorda bay. This French colony was soon abandoned, to be sure, but it had its influence upon the Spaniards who, beginning in earnest in 1690, established the chain of *missions, presidios* and *pueblos* that were to be the bulwark of a colonization program that lasted unabated throughout the next century.

Spanish-Colonial Buildings in Texas
(Those starred the more important architecturally)

Building	Date of Foundation	Building	Date of Foundation
San Miguel de Soccoro, near El Paso ...	1681	San Francisco de los Tejas (near Crockett)	1690
San Antonio de los Tiguas, Isleta ... ... (Later called Corpus Christi de los Tiguas, now called Nuestra Señora del Carmen)	1681	(Later reëstablished as San Francisco de los Neches, which in turn was later reëstablished as San Francisco de la Espada)	
San Cristobal (on Chonchas River near Presidio)	1683	Santissimo Nombre de Maria (on Neches River)	1690
San Francisco de Julimes (near Presidio)	1683	San Juan Bautista (on Rio Grande near Eagle Pass)	1699

[1] Don Juan de Oñate and the Founding of New Mexico. New Mex. Hist. Rev. Vol. I, 42.

Building	Date of Foundation
San Francisco de los Neches (on Neches River)	1716
San José de los Nazones (near Nacogdoches)	1716
(Later reëstablished as San Juan de Capistrano)	
La Purísima Concepción de los Asinai (near Nacogdoches)	1716
Nuestra Señora de la Guadalupe (near Nacogdoches)	1716
San Antonio de Padua (San Antonio)	1716
Nuestra Señora de los Dolores	1717
*San Antonio de Valero (Alamo), San Antonio	1718
(Formed of a merging of San Ildefonso, originally on the Mexican side of the Rio Grande, and San Antonio de Padua)	
*San José y San Miguel de Aguayo, near San Antonio	1720
(Recently restored by Harvey P. Smith, Architect)	
San Francisco Xavier de Naxera, San Antonio	1722
Espiritu Santo, Goliad	1722
(Originally on the site of La Salle's fort on Matagorda Bay, removed in 1749 to Goliad)	
*San Francisco de la Espada, near San Antonio	1731
*San Juan de Capistrano, near San Antonio	1731

Building	Date of Foundation
*La Purísima Concepción de Acuña, San Antonio	1731
*Church of San Fernando, San Antonio	1734
San Francisco Xavier, near Rockdale ...	1746
Nuestra Señora de la Candelaria, near Rockdale	1749
San Ildefonso, near Rockdale	1749
*Old Spanish Governor's House, San Antonio	1749
(Restored by Harvey P. Smith, Architect)	
*Nuestra Señora del Rosario, near Goliad	1754
Nuestra Señora de la Luz, near mouth of Trinity River	1756
Nuestra Señora de la Guadalupe, northeast of San Antonio	1757
San Saba, on headwaters of San Saba River	1757
Santa Cruz, on headwaters of San Saba River	1757
Nuestra Señora de Guadalupe, San Saba River	1757
Nuestra Señora de la Candelaria, San Saba River	1762
San Lorenzo, on headwaters of Nueces River	1762
Refugio, mouth of San Antonio River (later moved)	1791

A study of such structures among those above listed as are still standing reveals the following architectural traits.

Materials of Construction : Adobe (sun-dried) bricks, burned bricks, and stone, laid in lime-and-sand mortar, formed the principal materials of construction in Texas.

Architectural Characteristics : A. Plans. Buildings generally arranged in such a way that, with the additional high walls, they formed an enclosure to which gates gave access. Water from a well or a creek, led through the walls, gave a domestic supply. Arcades did not completely surround the court but were used in front of the convent or other important structure. The church was usually at one side and a granary was amongst the important structures. Churches were simple basilican or cruciform (La Purísima Concepción) with double towers at the facade of a pierced belfry crowning the facade.

B. Roofs, especially on churches, were formed of low masonry domes or tunnel vaults, while minor structures were covered with low pitched roofs of timber construction. Such domes were generally invisible in perspective except at the crossing where they were elevated on drums and crowned by a lantern.

C. Belfries were of two types: (a) a heavy, square tower surmounted by an arched belfry with dome and lantern, as at Mission San José y San Miguel de Aguayo, La Purísima Concepción and San Antonio de Valero (Alamo) for which towers were apparently originally planned: (b) a pierced belfry as at Missions San Juan de Capistrano or San Francisco de la Espada.

D. Walls were of heavy masonry, bare and unadorned except upon facades or around openings. Windows were round-headed, pointed, or upon occasion, elaborately outlined.

The decorative doors at Missions San Francisco de la Espada and San José y San Miguel de Aguayo and the elaborately carved decorative windows and niches at San José y Miguel de Aguayo or San Antonio de Valero illustrate the variety attained in these features of the architecture.

E. Interiors were generally quite splendid, although they are not well preserved today. La Purísima Concepción and the restored San José y San Miguel de Aguayo offer some notion of the original condition, however.

V. Spanish-Colonial Architecture in New Mexico

Although Fray Marcos de Niza discovered New Mexico as early as 1539 and Coronado explored the territory between 1540 and 1542, the actual settlement of the area did not take place until 1598 when that intrepid explorer and founder, Don Juan de Oñate, arrived with four hundred colonists—men, women and children—eighty-three ox-wagons and several hundred cattle to take up life in the wilderness—the first European settlement in America any great distance from the coast. Oñate had outfitted the expedition at a tremendous cost, the expense of which he was able to bear out of the wealth derived from the silver mines at Zacatecas in Mexico.

Establishing a settlement near the present site of San Juan *pueblo*, Oñate set out to explore the central territories. In 1604—5 with thirty men he made a trip across the deserts to the Gulf of California, a distance of nine hundred miles and back. There developed, however, dissatisfaction with his administration of New Mexican affairs and in August of 1607 Oñate was forced to resign as governor. For a time the fate of New Mexico was in the balance but at length (1609) Don Pedro de Peralta was appointed, thus marking a new era in the development of the province. "The day of the get-rich-quick *adelantado* was over, and a settled policy of gradual development at royal expense was inaugurated," says Dr. George P. Hammond.[1]

During the first year of his administration Governor Peralta carried out the instructions from Mexico to proceed to the founding of *La Villa Real de Santa Fé de San Francisco* (the Royal Chartered Town of the Holy Faith of St. Francis), the capital and the forerunner of the modern Santa Fé. From this capital the grey-robed Franciscan friars trudged hundreds of footsore miles to convert the Indians and establish the missions that were to form the backbone of colonization in the province and eventually to coin a new architectural vernacular.

In 1617 only a few of the original Oñate party remained but in 1630 Benavides reported a Spanish population of two hundred-fifty and seven hundred Mexican Indians who in the wake of the Spaniards had entered the province. In 1680 there was a fierce uprising of the *Pueblo* Indians and it is estimated that some four hundred of the twenty-five hundred Spaniards, including twenty-two Franciscan *padres*, were killed. A thousand survivors in Santa Fé were besieged in the Palace of the Governors

[1] The Founding of New Mexico—New Mex. Hist. Rev. Vol. II, 143.

[29]

for a week, at the end of which time they attacked their besiegers killing three hundred of them and capturing fifty more whom they hanged in the *Plaza*. The next day the Spaniards fought their way to freedom and retreated across the state to El Paso.

Twelve years later (1692) Don Diego de Vargas reconquered New Mexico and recaptured Santa Fé, and in December of the next year with eight hundred colonists, he resettled the capital and brought permanent peace to the land.

It is impossible to mention all the examples which delineate the Spanish-Colonial style in New Mexico, those upon which the analysis of the style is based, however, are named below:

Important Examples :

Building	Date of Foundation
San Juan de los Caballeros (present church later)	1598
Socorro (Nuestra Señora del Socorro)	1598
(Present church dates from 1615 — 1620; rebuilt and still in use)	
Nambé (San Francisco)	1598
Santa Ana	1607
Taos (San Geronimo, now in ruins (*circa*)	1600
Santo Domingo (Old church undermined by river; present church dates from 1886)	1607
Palace of the Governors, Santa Fé ...	1609
(Rebuilt after the insurrection of 1680 and many times since)	
Pecos (Old church ruined)	1617
Jemez (San Diego) (church ruined) ...	1617
Picuris (San Lorenzo)	1620
Isleta (San Antonio) ... ... before	1629
(church described by Benavides, in 1630, as "costly and beautiful")	
Zuñi (church unroofed) ... ... before	1629
Santa Clara	1629
Abó (church in ruins)	1629
Ácoma (San Stephano) (on table rock 350 feet above the plain)	1629
Tabira (the famous Gran Quivira, now in ruins)	1629

Building	Date of Foundation
Zia (Nuestra Señora de la Asunción) before	1630
Santa Ana ... ... before	1630
Tesuque (San Diego) ... ... before	1630
San Felipe (present church dates from 1700—1725) ... ... before	1630
Sandía (San Francisco) early centre destroyed in 1680, present church (ruined), 1748)	1680
Cochití (San Buenaventura) church here before	1680
Santa Cruz, Spanish Church	1695
San Ildefonso	1696
Laguna (San José)	1699
Ranchos de Taos (Probably not a mission) church dates from	1772
The Churches of Santa Fé	
Mission San Miguel (often dated 1541, now thought to have been built 1607, destroyed 1680, rebuilt 1710, restored 1888)	1607
Church of San Francisco (Not a mission; replaced by the cathedral) ...	1627
Church of Our Lady of Guadalupe (Not a mission)	1640
Capilla Rosario (Chapel of the Rosary)	1692
Church of Our Lady of Light (Castrense) (Not a mission)	1785
Sanctuario at Chimayó	1816

A study of the accompanying plates will acquaint the reader with the outstanding characteristics of the New Mexican Colonial, a worded description of which is attempted below.

Materials of Construction: *Adobe* bricks or stone, laid in mud-mortar and mud-plastered inside and out, formed the principal materials of construction. Roofs were of heavy beams, wood-ceiled and covered with turf.

Architectural Characteristics: A. Plans. The mission structures were grouped about a *patio* or "*plazita*" (little plaza), the church forming one side, the domestic buildings enclosing the other three sides. Churches were one-aisled, basilican or simple cruciform in plan. The front was usually flanked by double towers or surmounted by a pierced belfry. Such facades often carried a balcony or upper porch at the choir-loft level, as at Tesuque, Santo Domingo or Cochití.

B. The general lines of these structures resemble the terraced Pueblo Indian houses, building up into picturesque natural masses with flowing lines indicating hand smoothing of the mud-plaster with which they were covered.

C. Belfries were of two types: (a) the simple, coupled, square towers, crowned by open belfries, as at Ácoma, Santa Cruz, Isleta, San Felipe, Pecos (now ruined), Zuñi (ruined) and elsewhere: (b) a pierced belfry above the facade wall of the church, as at Laguna, Zia, San Juan de los Caballeros, Nambé, Santa Clara, Picuris, Arroyo Hondo (Taos County), Cochití and others.

D. Walls were blank, bare and unadorned, even at the front of the churches where only the towers and porches relieve the outline. Often a low parapet, surrounding the flat, invisible roof and pierced by "*canales*" (gargoyles) to permit drainage, crowned side and rear walls.

E. A feature of New Mexican architecture was the porch or covered walk ("*portales*"), not arcaded as in California, Arizona or Texas, but colonnaded and formed of heavy, carved, wooden beams and brackets ("*vigas*") resting upon round, wooden columns. Such beams were often notched, chamferred or carved and relieved by color. An excellent example of such *portales* is to be seen at the restored Palace of the Governors in Santa Fé.

F. Interiors were generally blank and bare except at the sanctuary end of the churches where gaudily painted *retablos* and altars concentrated religious interest. Paintings, brought from Spain or Mexico, often relieved the bare interiors, while the carved *vigas* of the roof and choir contributed their quota of interest. Upon occasion painted dadoes adorned church interiors.

VI. Spanish-Colonial Architecture in Arizona

Although the mission architecture of Arizona is largely attributable to Franciscan zeal and industry, the early endeavors at colonization and Christianization of that area were of Jesuit origin. *Padre* Eusebio Kino first visited the site of the future San Xavier del Bac (Queen of the Arizona missions) in 1692 and again in 1699. It was probably at this latter date that he determined upon a foundation at this point, for the next year he returned to Bac and founded the mission of San Xavier, calling it in honor of the great Jesuit "Apostle to the Indies."

As is related earlier in this volume, the Jesuits were called from their labors by the order of expulsion promulgated 1767 and the missions of Arizona, together with those formerly administered by the order in northern Mexico and *Baja* California, were turned over to other hands. Those in Arizona fell to the Franciscans.

The Arizona missions were terminal posts on a chain of establishments mainly in Old Mexico. Of the seven or eight missions once in Arizona, only San Xavier remains in anything like good condition. Some have all but completely disappeared while the balance are in ruins. Below is listed those structures presumably established as full-fledged missions. There were of course in addition to these a number of *visitas* (calling points) and *asistencias* (contributing chapels).

Spanish Colonial Examples in Arizona

Building	Date of Foundation	Building	Date of Foundation
San Gabriel de Guevavi (utterly ruined)	1692	San Xavier del Bac	1700
San Cayetano de Calabazas (ruined) ...	1694	(Much restored but in a way in keeping with the ancient work; the supreme example of the style in Arizona)	
San José de Tumacácori (partially ruined)	1697	San José del Tucson (ruined)	1776
San Augustín del Oyaut (ruined)	1699	Santa Gertrudis de Tubac (ruined)	

Upon Mission San Xavier and the ruins of San José de Tumacácori the catalog of architectural features listed below has largely been based.

Materials of construction consisted mainly of *adobe* bricks or burned bricks. Roofs and domes as well as walls, in the more important examples, were of burned bricks; walls in less important examples of *adobe*. Stucco was generally used to cover all walls and domes.

[32]

Architectural Characteristics: A. Plans. Buildings were, as elsewhere, disposed around an enclosure *(patio)*, the church forming one side, as at San Xavier del Bac. Churches were either basilican or cruciform in plan with double towers at the front, as at San Xavier, or with a single tower at side, as at Tumacácori (ruined).

B. Walls were massive, heavy and unadorned except the facades of churches which were often treated with modelled plaster decoration in full color. The supreme example of such decoration is the matchless San Xavier del Bac.

C. Terraced bell towers are found at San Xavier and Tumacácori (ruined).

D. Curved gables were used at San Xavier and Tumacácori (no longer in place).

E. Excellent vaulted and domical roofs are to be seen at San Xavier, where the cruciform church is covered with five low domes, the sixth, that at the crossing, being raised on a drum and therefore visible in perspective. These domes are carried on pendentives.

F. Elaborately carved *retablos* and gilded colorful altars, very rich and oriental in effect, imparted an intense opulence to such interiors which were generally in full color.

VII. Spanish-Colonial Architecture in California

When, in 1769, Don Gaspár de Portolá and *Padre* Junípero Serra set out for *Alta* California, a new chapter in Franciscan missionary activity in what is now the United States was opening. In spite of the fact that this was the last of these socio-religious movements participated in by the soldiery and priesthood of Old Spain, it was to be in many respects the most successful. As compared with Texas, New Mexico and Arizona, Nature has been prodigal in her allotment of virtues to California for here the western winds breathe throughout the year a genial warmth over the land, forming of the California coast a country that in many respects resembles the Spanish homeland, the climate of San Francisco, with its chill winds and fog resembling that of Burgos, while the climate of San Diego is strikingly reminiscent of that of Seville or Barcelona.

San Diego de Alcalá, near the present city of San Diego, was the first mission to be established. The foundation was accomplished in July, 1769, by *Padre* Serra, *padre-presidente* of the Missions of *Alta* California, who the next year founded Mission San Carlos de Morromeo on Monterey Bay. San Diego and Monterey marked the boundaries of the first Spanish missionary endeavors in California but the intervening territory was filled in rapid succession with flourishing establishments. It is said that it was the intention to have the missions located a day's journey apart along the coast trail known as *El Camino Real* (the royal highway), and seemingly the road was divided at about that interval. In all, there were twenty-one missions in California, together with several *asistencias* (contributing chapels), the *Presidio* Chapel *(La Capilla Real)* at Monterey and the Plaza Church at Los Ángeles.

Spanish-Colonial Examples in California
(Those architecturally outstanding are starred)

Building	Date of Foundation	Building	Date of Foundation
*San Diego de Alcalá	1769	Santa Clara de Asís	1777
*San Carlos de Borromeo (Carmel) ...	1770	*San Buenaventura	1782
*San Antonio de Padua	1771	*Santa Bárbara	1786
*San Gabriel Arcángel	1771	La Concepción Purísima	1787
Nuestra Señora de la Soledad	1771	Santa Cruz	1791
San Luis Obispo de Tolosa	1772	San Miguel Arcángel	1797
San Francisco de Asís	1776	*San Juan Bautista	1797
*San Juan Capistrano	1776	*San Fernando Rey de España	1797

Building	Date of Foundation	Building	Date of Foundation
San José de Guadalupe	1797	*La Capilla Real de Monterey* (Presidio Chapel)	1770
*San Luis Rey de Francia	1798	(Present church dates from 1794).	
*Santa Inés	1804	San Antonio de Pala (an asistencia of	
San Rafael Arcángel	1817	San Rey de Francia)	1816
San Francisco Solano	1823	Plaza Chapel at Los Ángeles	1822

An examination of the more important of the structures above listed yields the following data regarding the architecture. Materials of construction in use in California were *adobe* bricks, burned bricks, stone; burned tile for roofs, carried upon wooden beams. Many buildings made use of all these materials, stone being used for the church, bricks for the arcades and important structural parts, and *adobe* for the less important walls. Stucco or plaster was used as a universal exterior wall covering.

Architectural Characteristics: A. Plans: The structures were disposed around a *patio* with garden and fountain. This arrangement was followed or projected at every establishment, though not always completed. Good *patios* remain at San Luis Rey de Francia, San Juan Capistrano, Santa Bárbara, Santa Inés, San Juan Bautista and elsewhere.

B. Arcaded, cloister-like corridors surrounding *patios* or across the front of the buildings are to be seen at San Luis Rey de Francia, San Juan Capistrano, San Fernado Rey de España, Santa Bárbara, Santa Inés and San Juan Bautista.

C. Solid and massive walls, piers and buttresses were characteristic of the California structures. The buttress was used for two purposes: (a) to resist the lateral thrusts of arches or vaults, as at San Gabriel, the ruined church of San Juan Capistrano which was roofed by low stone domes, and San Carlos Borromeo, the nave of which was spanned by transverse arches which carried a vaulted roof; and (b) to make the walls more stable against earthquakes as at San Buenaventura, Santa Inés, Santa Bárbara and other places.

Walls were generally undecorated except around openings or upon the facade of the church where applied ornamentation was used.

D. Roofs with wide, projecting eaves, and low-sloping, red tile coverings, indicative of the heavy rainfall of the winter season, covered most of the structures.

E. Curved, pedimented gables were used, as at San Diego Alcalá (now restored), San Luis Rey de Francia, San Gabriel (belfry), Capilla Real (Monterey).

F. Terraced bell-towers with dome and lantern were used on the more important churches like San Luis Rey de Francia, San Juan Capistrano (now destroyed), Santa Bárbara, San Carlos Borromeo, but pierced belfries were also employed, as at San Antonio de Pala, San Gabriel, Santa Inés, San Diego de Alcalá (restored).

VIII. Present-Day Spanish-Colonial Architecture in the United States

In the foregoing pages we have traced the vari-colored architecture of Old Spain from its home-land, through Mexico into the various future American states, where, introduced by Spanish priests, soldiers and colonists, it took root and where, in response to new demands, as time went on, it produced unique, indigenous expressions. Had it not been for the "accident of history" that awarded this one-time Hispanic empire to an Anglo-Saxon race, perhaps there would never have been a break in architectural tradition of this area. As it happened, however, Mexico and her provinces north of the Rio Grande in time became independent of Spain, and Florida and the Gulf Coast were likewise lost to Spanish possession. In turn also, possessions on this side of the Rio Grande were lost by Mexico and the great Southwest witnessed the advent of conquerors of entirely different blood, history and ideals.

These Yankees from the Atlantic Seaboard for a time tried to make the American Colonial and its derivatives give expression to life in these great open spaces still largely peopled by descendants of the original Spanish stock and the Mexicans who, during the long Spanish regime, had drifted into the country. In some sections as in Santa Fé, New Mexico, and around Monterey, California, (especially in the so-called Monterey Style) there was an eventual blending of the Spanish and Yankee styles that resulted in some charming forms, but on the whole the frigid, wood-begotten New England types were poorly adapted, climatically and historically, to reflect the type of life and living developed in these semi-arid, sun-lit lands of the Old Southwest.

Little by little the incongruity of attempting to make these "foreign" forms express the life and thought in this vast Hispanic domain dawned upon architect and layman alike with the result that, within the past quarter century, there has grown up in each of these states a staunch regard for these fine old structures and a real desire to make them, through the beautifully appropriate precedent which they afford, the inspiration of new architectural work, both private and public.

Each of these states now has energetic protagonists of these old regional expressions who, grounding themselves thoroughly in archaeological investigation, are available to "restore" those old structures which, through the neglect of man and the onslaught of the elements, have fallen into disrepair.

In California organizations like the Landmarks Club and similar groups, to say nothing of the Church, have long been at work safeguarding and restoring these fine old reminders of our Hispanic past. Like movements are on foot in the other states, that in Texas which resulted first in the restoration of the Old Governor's Palace in San Antonio and recently in the complete restoration of Mission San José y Miguel de Aguayo near San Antonio (both carried out by Harvey Partridge Smith, Architect) being particularly progressive.

Of course the whole value of such restorations artistically is to perpetuate the knowledge as to what these fine old forms really were. But out of this has come also the realization of how sensibly appropriate they are to the land of their inception. As a result, many in these states have wished to build in the Spanish Colonial rather than in the American Colonial. And architects have been found ready and eager to carry out new work "in the spirit of the old", but as sanely adapted to modern life and living as the old was adapted to the pattern of life in the day in which it was erected. Thus, as in the old days, there grew up in each of these well-defined provinces a unique and indigenous expression, so today each of these modern states is forging its own regional vernacular based upon life in its particular sector.

For a while there was a tendency to trade styles, so to speak, and one would find California Spanish Colonial in Texas and along the railway lines in New Mexixo and Arizona. Once the author discovered a New Mexican *pueblo*-type house as far out of its habitat as Florida, but today each of these regions is attempting to express itself in its own variant of this versatile sun-loving style. A study of the succeeding plates will acquaint one with the success that has been attained.

In a land so tropical as is Florida where all sorts of citrus trees and the jessamine, oleander, almond, banana and palm flourish, a sunny Spanish architecture is perfectly appropriate. Here the architects, basing their work upon the more florid types of the Spanish Colonial, have modified these forms by infiltrations from Moorish Spain and North Africa and by importations from the Mexican Spanish Colonial from across the Rio Grande. But from whatever source the inspiration, a general Hispanic character has been achieved that is as expressive of life in present-day Florida as was the Spanish work of another day.

In modern work along the Gulf Coast, a certain mingling of forms—part Spanish, part French—is to be found, an eloquent tell-tale of the varied and capricious history of this area which was alternately under the banner of France and of Spain before it finally became American territory.

In Texas certainly the long Franciscan tradition and the extant mission monuments have indelibly marked the work of our time. A glance at such a structure as the

[37]

Missouri, Kansas and Texas Station in San Antonio (Plate 100) will prove the potency of such precedent. On the other hand, in the residences of Texas one catches a distinct modern note. One feels that these are homes of today but definitely in the tradition of eighteenth century Texas. That they are in no sense archaeological parrot-phrases of the past is to be noted and commended.

The Spanish Colonial of New Mexico is perhaps the most distinctive of all the American Hispanic types. This is due to the large amount of Indian influence which the style incorporates. Coming into a land peopled by sedentary Indians living in well built and picturesque *pueblos* (villages), the *padres* utilized the Indian craftsmen to erect their churches and houses. The *padres* maintained Spanish utilities, arrangements and proportions but permitted the Indians to erect the buildings in their own traditional methods of construction. Thus we get an architecture half-Spanish, half-Indian, the suave sinuous lines of which are reflected in such fine modern works as the Museum of New Mexico or the Laboratory of Anthropology, both in Santa Fé.

In New Mexico this style is sometimes called Pueblo Architecture, but it is as often called the Santa Fé School. The presence in Santa Fé and at Albuquerque of schools of archaeology, anthropology and southwestern research has naturally generated a regard for all the past manifestations of the human spirit. Thus in New Mexico the old is loved, cherished and revered as precedent for the current buildings that are arising on all sides. And a great amount of really excellent work has already been accomplished.

Naturally some examples, more-or-less theatrical and bizarre, are upon occasion encountered but this is only to be expected when builders, imitating the work of trained architects, attempt to use a style that requires intense and prolonged research. But New Mexico suffers in this respect to a lesser degree than does Florida and California where the influence of the "movie lot" is felt and high-pressure real estate promoters have capitalized upon the popularity of the movement.

In Arizona, the clean, trim "desert" forms of San Xavier de Bac near Tucson embody a noble tradition for churches, schools and other public buildings and to an extent such precedent has been utilized, but Arizona architects have been less alive to the fine indigenous precedent of their own state than one would expect and only recently has work in the true Arizonan manner begun to appear. We show only one example, the remodelled Cathedral of Saint Augustine at Tucson, the work of Henry O. Jaastad, a pioneer in the appreciation of Arizonan regional forms.

California, on the other hand, with its wide range of climate, its long mission history, its unique mountain-desert-maritime geography and its varied flora, has been very responsive to historic precedent and has made the most of it. Here, to be sure, the simplest of forms are enhanced by a wonderfully clear and vibrant atmosphere and the deep shadows induced by a vivid sunshine make unnecessary the elaborate forms, the modelled and carved details and the color so acceptable in Texas or Arizona. This fundamental simplicity makes it possible to develop a delightfully varied domestic architecture with the fewest of expedients. In this respect California enjoys something of an artistic handicap over her less-favored neighbors and thus Californian architects have given us a modern Hispanic architecture expressed with a restraint that is as frugal, straight-forward and craftsmanlike as the old mission houses, the simple masses of which to this day make such glorious pictures under California's white sun.

Plate 1

Doorway

Tower Detail

The Old Cathedral Saint Augustine, Florida
(Photographs by Wolfe)

General View from the Plaza

Plate 2

Matansas River Side

Bridge and Moat

Sentry Post

Bird's-Eye View of the Fort   *(Photos. by Wolfe)*

Old Spanish Castle San Marco (now Fort Marion), Saint Augustine, Florida

Plate 3

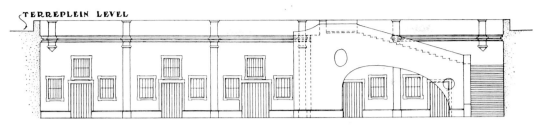

EAST WALL OF PLAZA

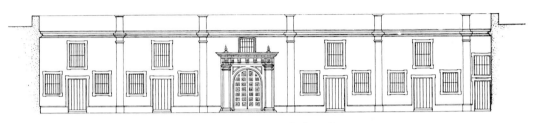

NORTH WALL OF PLAZA

SCALE IN FEET

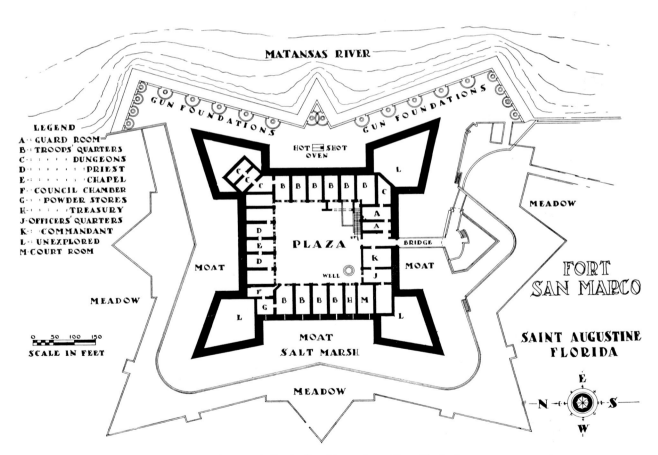

Old Spanish Castle San Marco (now Fort Marion)
Saint Augustine, Florida

Plate 4

Old Spanish Slave Market, Saint Augustine, Florida

Old Spanish Gate
Saint Augustine, Florida. (Photos. by Wolfe)

Plate 5

Mission San Antonio de Valero (Alamo), San Antonio, Texas
(Photo. by Summerville)

Plate 6

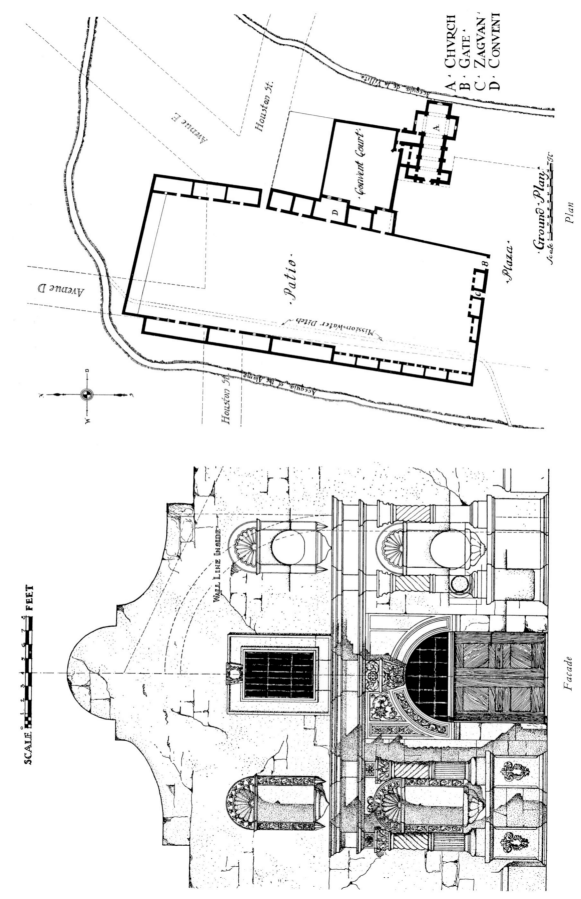

A · CHVRCH
B · GATE ·
C · ZAGVAN ·
D · CONVENT

Avenue E

Houston St.

Convent Court

Ground-Plan·
Scale

Plan

Patio·

Avenue D

Mission Water Ditch

Acequia of the Alamo

Houston St.

Plaza·

B

SCALE FEET

WALL LINE INSIDE

Facade

Mission San Antonio de Valero (Alamo) San Antonio, Texas

Plate 7

Mission San Antonio de Valero (Alamo) San Antonio, Texas
(Photo. by Putnam Studios)

Plate 8

Facade
(*Photo. by Putnam Studios*)

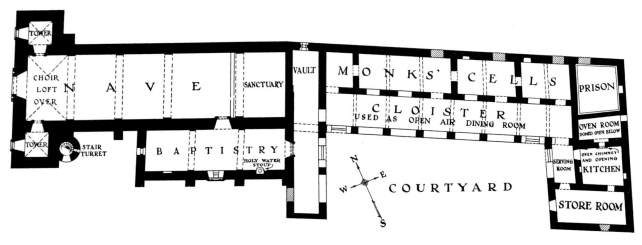

Plan

Mission San José y San Miguel de Aguayo, near San Antonio, Texas

Plate 9

Doorway. — Mission San José y San Miguel, near San Antonio, Texas
(Photo. by Putnam Studios)

Plate 10

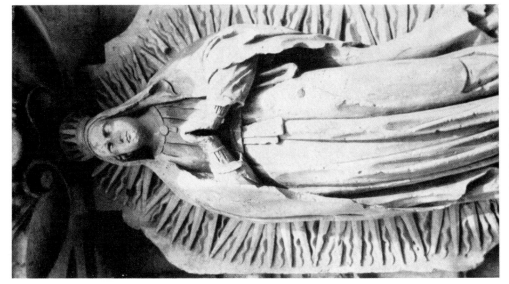

Detail of Our Lady of Guadalupe

Church Doorway

Detail of Carving around Doorway

Mission San José y San Miguel de Aguayo, near San Antonio, Texas

(Photos. by Atlee B. Ayres)

Plate 11

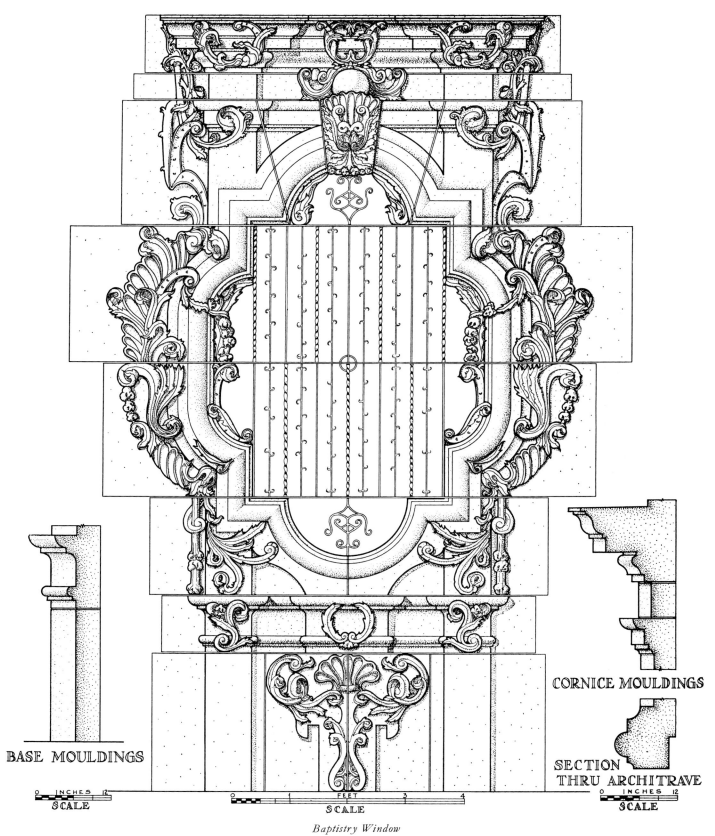

BASE MOULDINGS

CORNICE MOULDINGS

SECTION THRU ARCHITRAVE

Baptistry Window

Mission San José y San Miguel de Aguayo, near San Antonio, Texas

Plate 12

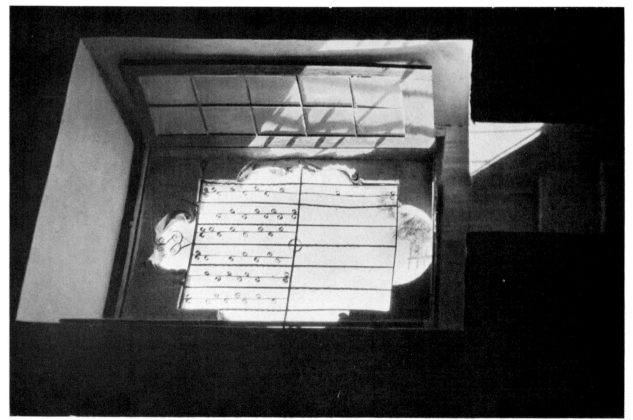

Baptistry Window—Exterior

Baptistry Window—Interior

Mission San José y San Miguel de Aguayo, near San Antonio, Texas

(Photos. by Atlee B. Ayres)

Plate 13

Ruined Church and Tower
Mission San José y Miguel de Aguayo near San Antonio, Texas

(Photo. by Putnam Studios)

Plate 14

Cloister

Side of Church and Tower

Cloister Detail

Mission San José y San Miguel de Aguayo, near San Antonio, Texas

(Photos. by Atlee B. Ayres)

Plate 15

Rear Door of Baptistry — Exterior

*Rear Door of Baptistry — Interior
Looking Toward Cloister*

Side Door of Baptistry

Mission San José y San Miguel de Aguayo, near San Antonio, Texas
(Photos. by Atlee B. Ayres)

Plate 16

Baptistry. — *San José y San Miguel de Aguayo, near San Antonio, Texas*
(Photo. by Harvey Patterson)

Plate 17

Mission Nuestra Señora de la Purísima Concepción de Acuña, San Antonio, Texas
(Copyrighted Photo. by Harvey Patterson)

Plate 18

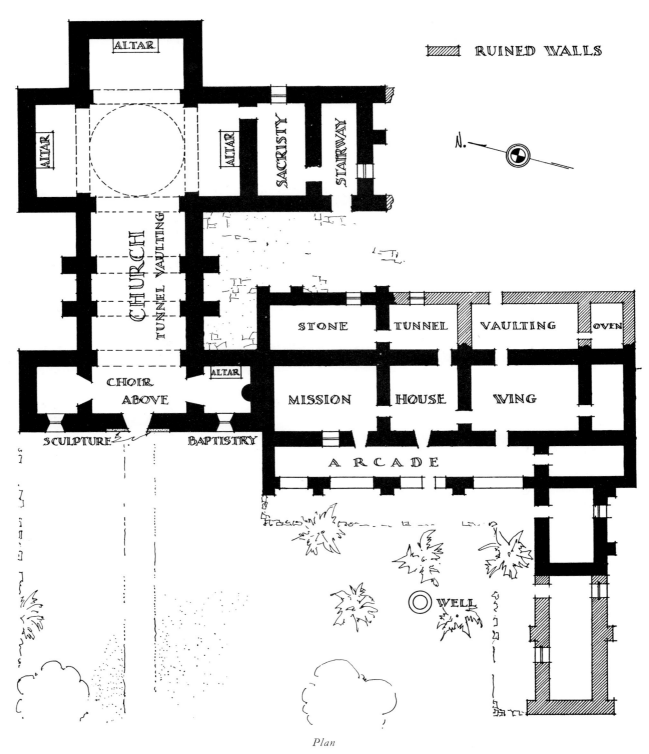

RUINED WALLS

ALTAR

ALTAR

ALTAR

SACRISTY

STAIRWAY

N.

CHURCH

TUNNEL VAULTING

STONE TUNNEL VAULTING OVEN

CHOIR

ABOVE

ALTAR

MISSION HOUSE WING

SCULPTURE

BAPTISTRY

ARCADE

WELL

Plan

Mission Nuestra Señora de la Purísima Concepción de Acuña, San Antonio, Texas

Plate 19

Facade of the Church

Towers from the Side of the Church

Tower and Dome at the Crossing

Mission Nuestra Señora de la Purísima Concepción de Acuña, San Antonio, Texas

(Photo. by Atlee B. Ayres and Harvey Patterson)

Plate 20

Interior of Church Looking toward Choir Loft

Doorway of the Church

Mission Nuestra Señora de la Purísima Concepción de Acuña, San Antonio, Texas. (*Photo. by Alice B. Ayres*)

Plate 21

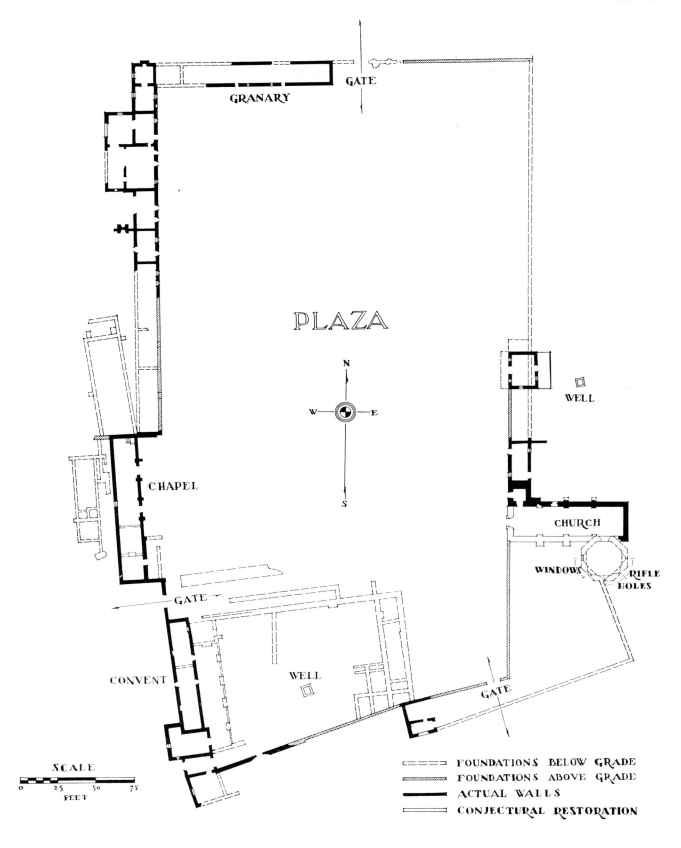

GATE

GRANARY

PLAZA

N

W · E

S

CHAPEL

WELL

CHURCH

WINDOWS — RIFLE HOLES

GATE

CONVENT

WELL

GATE

SCALE

0   25   50   75
FEET

⌐===⌐ FOUNDATIONS BELOW GRADE
▨▨▨ FOUNDATIONS ABOVE GRADE
▬▬▬ ACTUAL WALLS
☐☐☐ CONJECTURAL RESTORATION

MISSION SAN JUAN DE CAPISTRANO

Plan
Mission San Juan de Capistrano, near San Antonio, Texas

Plate 22

Side View of the Church (Courtesy of J. B. Lippincott Co.)

Belfry. — Mission San Juan de Capistrano, San Antonio, Texas (Photos by Harvey Patterson)

Plate 23

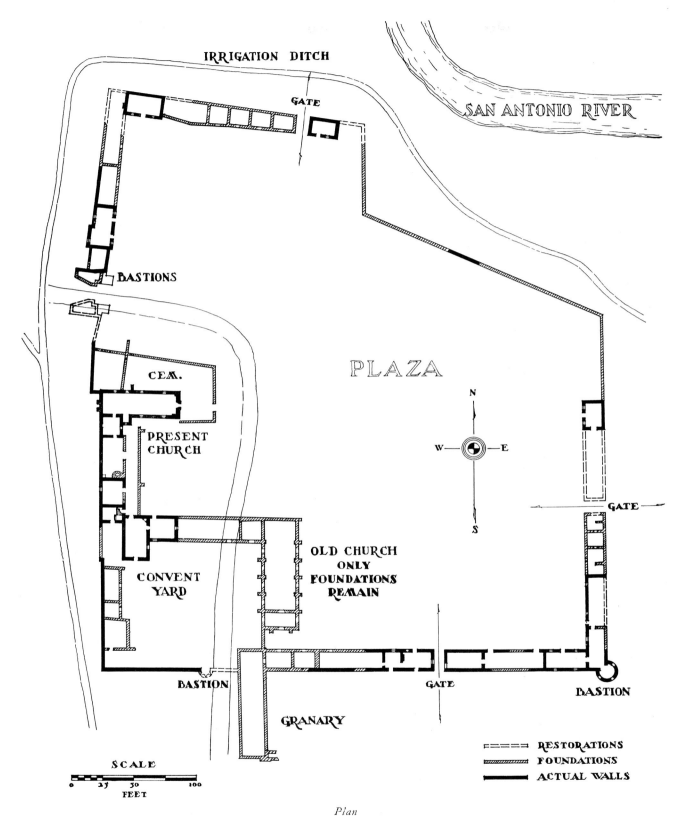

IRRIGATION DITCH

GATE

SAN ANTONIO RIVER

BASTIONS

PLAZA

CEM.

N

PRESENT
CHURCH

W — E

S

GATE

OLD CHURCH
ONLY
FOUNDATIONS
REMAIN

CONVENT
YARD

BASTION

GATE

BASTION

GRANARY

SCALE

0   25   50   100
FEET

RESTORATIONS
FOUNDATIONS
ACTUAL WALLS

Plan
Mission San Francisco de la Espada, near San Antonio, Texas

Plate 24

Facade of the Church
Mission San Francisco de la Espada near San Antonio, Texas

(Phot. by Harvey Patterson)

Plate 25

Church Doorway

Detail of the Facade

Mission San Francisco de la Espada, near San Antonio, Texas
(Photos. by Atlee B. Ayres)

Detail of Belfry

Plate 26

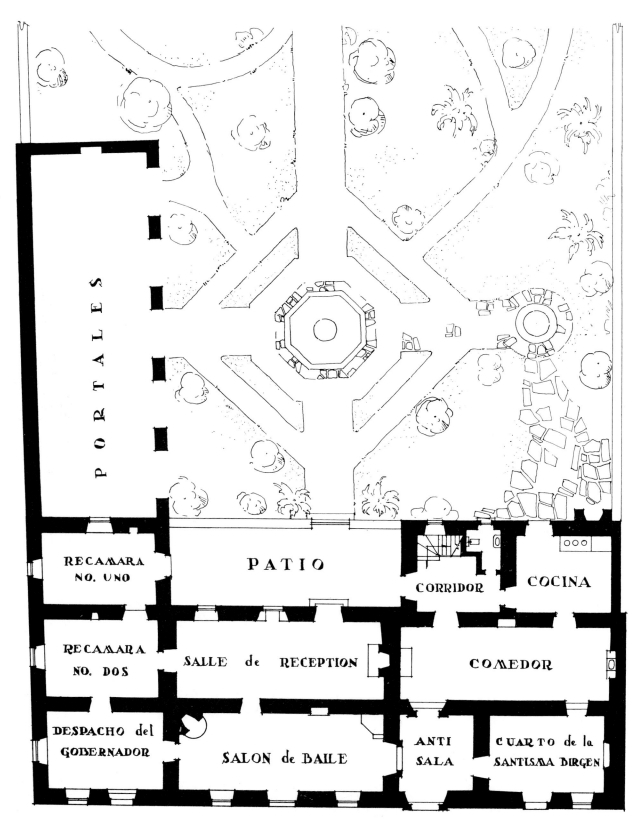

RECAMARA NO. UNO

RECAMARA NO. DOS

DESPACHO del GOBERNADOR

PORTALES

PATIO

SALLE de RECEPTION

SALON de BAILE

CORRIDOR

COCINA

COMEDOR

ANTI SALA

CUARTO de la SANTISMA BIRGEN

Plan

Old Spanish Governor's Palace, San Antonio, Texas

(Restoration by Harvey P. Smith, Architect)

Plate 27

Facade

Courtyard, looking toward kitchen from well. (Restoration by Harvey P. Smith, Architect)

Old Spanish Governor's Palace, San Antonio, Texas (Photos. by Harvey Patterson)

Plate 28

Stairway

Doorway

Old Spanish Governor's Palace, San Antonio, Texas

(Restoration by Harvey P. Smith, Architect) *Photos by Harvey Patterson.*

Plate 29

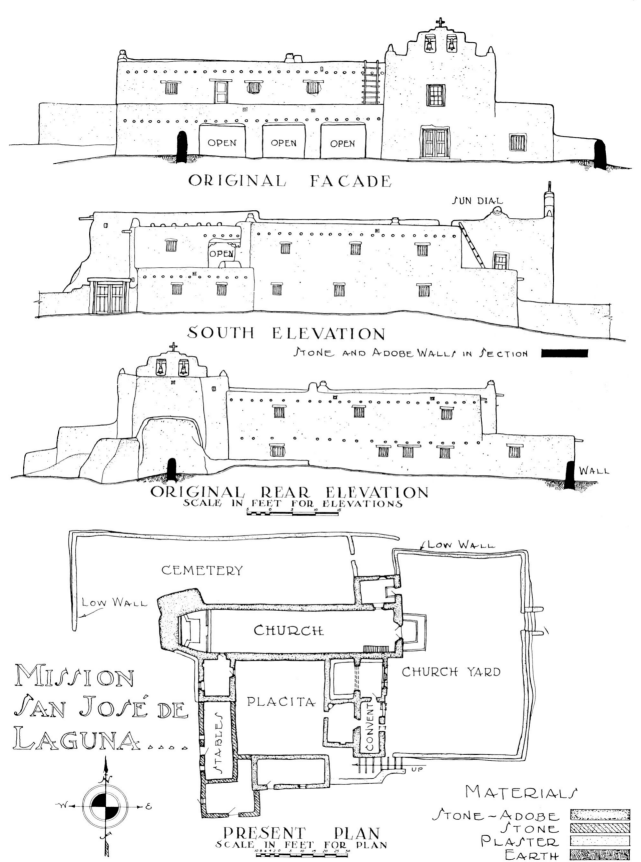

ORIGINAL FACADE

SOUTH ELEVATION

Stone and Adobe Walls in Section

ORIGINAL REAR ELEVATION
SCALE IN FEET FOR ELEVATIONS

SUN DIAL

WALL

CEMETERY

LOW WALL

LOW WALL

CHURCH

CHURCH YARD

PLACITA

STABLES

CONVENT

UP

MISSION SAN JOSÉ DE LAGUNA....

W E

PRESENT PLAN
SCALE IN FEET FOR PLAN

MATERIALS
STONE-ADOBE
STONE
PLASTER
EARTH

Mission San José de Laguna, Laguna Pueblo, New Mexico

Plate 30

General View   *(Photo. Taken some years ago)*

Roof of Church

Rear of the Church   *Side of Church*

Mission San José de Laguna, Laguna Pueblo, New Mexico   *(Photos. by Author)*

Plate 31

Tesuque Mission from a Painting by Carlos Vierra

Church at Pueblo Santo Domingo

Mission Church at Nambé Pueblo (now destroyed)

New Mexican Missions (Photos. by School of American Research)

Plate 32

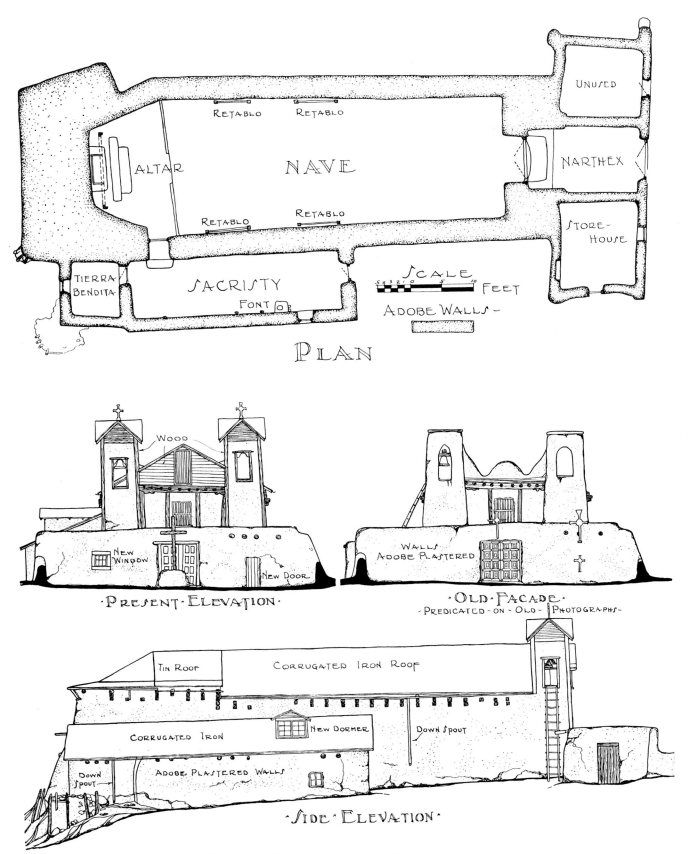

RETABLO   RETABLO

ALTAR   NAVE

RETABLO   RETABLO

UNUSED

NARTHEX

STORE-HOUSE

SCALE
5 4 3 2 1 0   5   10   FEET
ADOBE WALLS —

TIERRA BENDITA   SACRISTY   FONT

PLAN

WOOD

NEW WINDOW   NEW DOOR

·PRESENT·ELEVATION·

WALLS ADOBE PLASTERED

·OLD·FACADE·
·PREDICATED·ON·OLD·PHOTOGRAPHS·

TIN ROOF   CORRUGATED IRON ROOF

CORRUGATED IRON   NEW DORMER   DOWN SPOUT

DOWN SPOUT   ADOBE PLASTERED WALLS

·SIDE·ELEVATION·

El Santuario del Señor Esquipula at Chimayó, N. M.
Not a Mission but a Shrine for the Miraculous Cure of Disease

Plate 33

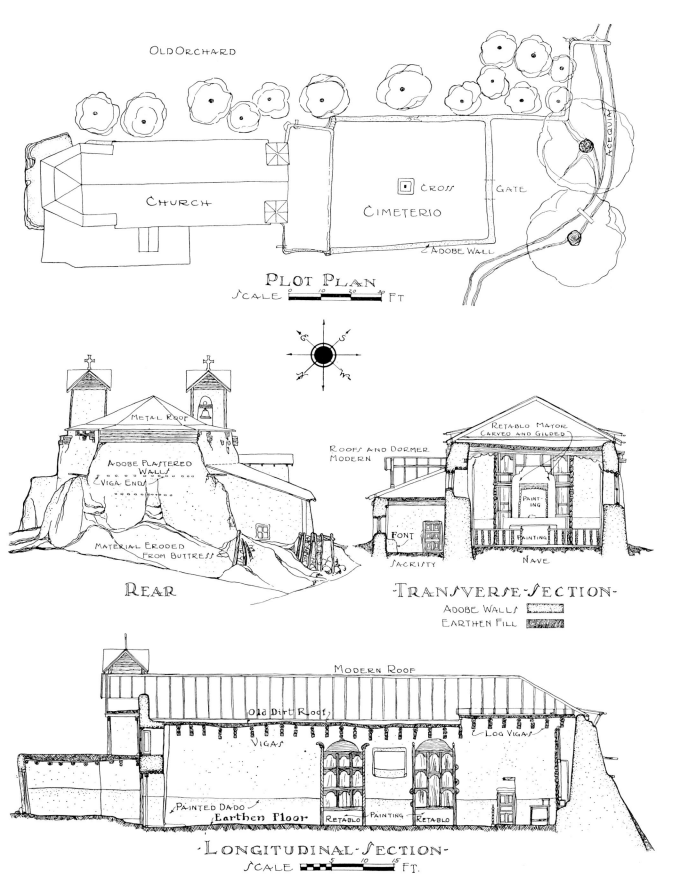

OLD ORCHARD

CHURCH

CROSS

GATE

CIMETERIO

ACEQUIA

ADOBE WALL

PLOT PLAN

SCALE 0 10 20 30 FT

REAR

METAL ROOF

ADOBE PLASTERED WALLS

VIGA ENDS

MATERIAL ERODED FROM BUTTRESS

TRANSVERSE SECTION

ROOFS AND DORMER MODERN

RETABLO MAYOR CARVED AND GILDED

PAINT-ING

FONT

PAINTING

SACRISTY

NAVE

ADOBE WALLS

EARTHEN FILL

LONGITUDINAL SECTION

MODERN ROOF

OLD DIRT ROOF

VIGAS

LOG VIGAS

PAINTED DADO

EARTHEN FLOOR

RETABLO

PAINTING

RETABLO

SCALE 5 10 15 FT.

El Santuario del Señor Esquipula at Chimayó, New Mexico

Plate 34

Interior View Looking toward Altar

Old Facade before Repairs were made   (Photos. by School of American Research)

El Santuario del Señor Esquipula at Chimayó, New Mexico

Plate 35

Door Detail

(*Photos, by School of American Research*)

Confessional

El Santuario del Señor Esquipula at Chimayó, New Mexico

Pulpit

Plate 36

Mission San Buenaventura de Cochití, New Mexico

Mission San Lorenzo at Picuris Pueblo, New Mexico

Church at Taos Pueblo, New Mexico
New Mexican Missions

(Photos. by School of American Research)

Plate 37

Mission Church at Santa Clara Pueblo, New Mexico

Mission Church at Ranchos de Taos, New Mexico

Plate 38

Rear Elevation

(Photos. by Author)

Towers and Buttresses

Mission Church at Ranchos de Taos, New Mexico

Plate 39

·THIS·DRAWING·BASED·ON·HISTORIC·AMERICAN·BUILDINGS·SURVEY·

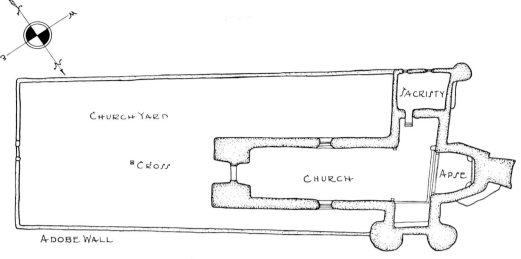

PLOT PLAN

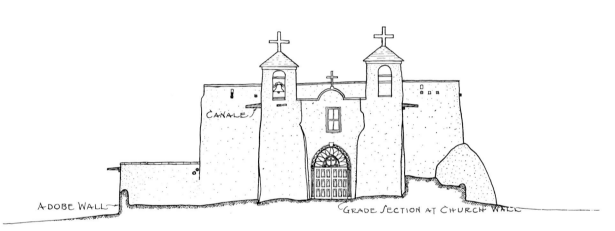

FRONT ELEVATION

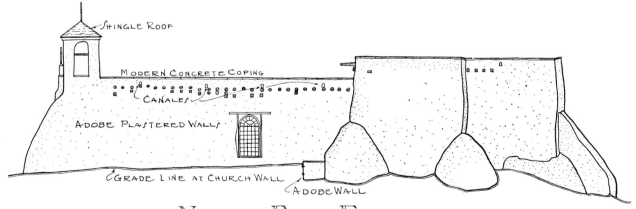

NORTH EAST ELEVATION

·MISSION·CHURCH·AT·RANCHOS·DE·TAOS·

Plate 40

Facade

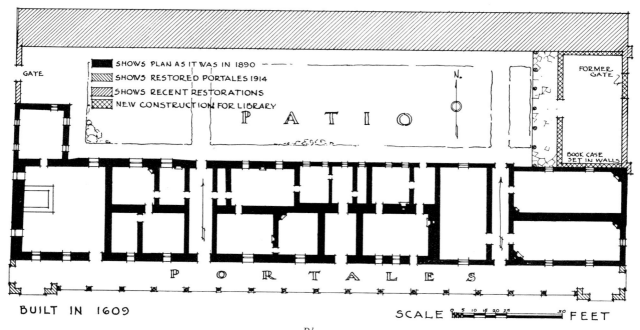

Plan

Palace of the Governors, Santa Fé, New Mexico

Plate 41

Ceiling of Women's Room, Art Museum, Santa Fé

Roof Construction, Art Museum, Santa Fé

A Rustic Portale

New Mexican Mission Architecture — Details

Beams in Church at San Ildefonso

Beam in Church at Santa Cruz

Plate 42

CHAMFER

FROM THE PALACE OF THE GOVERNORS
SANTA FÉ

NEW MEXICAN VIGAS

ROSARIO CHAPEL

SANCTUARIO DE N. S. DE GUADALUPE
SANTA FÉ

BEAM

MISSION AT LAGUNA

Modern Vigas–Patio–Museum–Santa Fé

Old Vigas, Mission at San Ildefonso

New Mexican Mission Architecture — Details

Plate 43

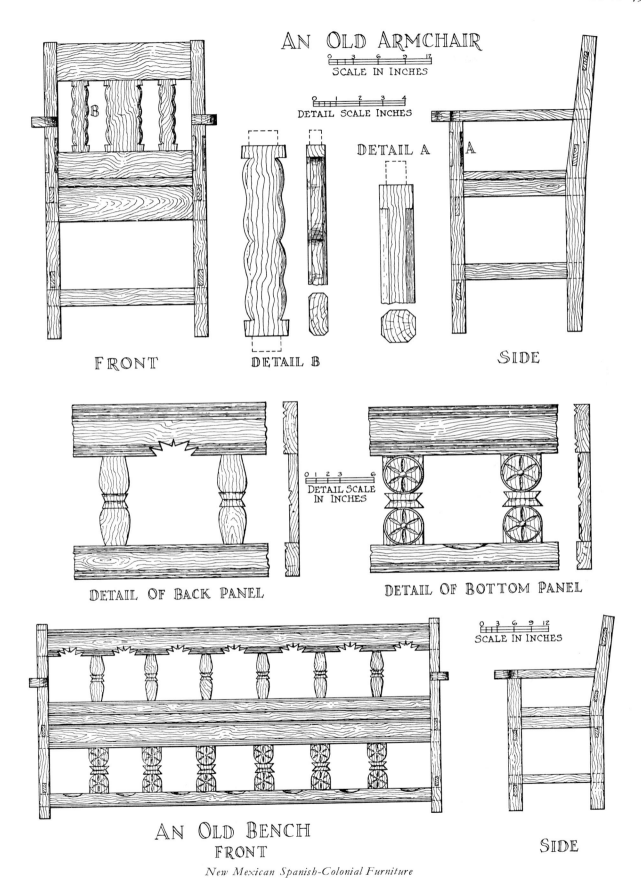

AN OLD ARMCHAIR

SCALE IN INCHES

DETAIL SCALE INCHES

DETAIL A

FRONT

DETAIL B

SIDE

DETAIL OF BACK PANEL

DETAIL SCALE IN INCHES

DETAIL OF BOTTOM PANEL

AN OLD BENCH

FRONT

SCALE IN INCHES

SIDE

New Mexican Spanish-Colonial Furniture

Plate 44

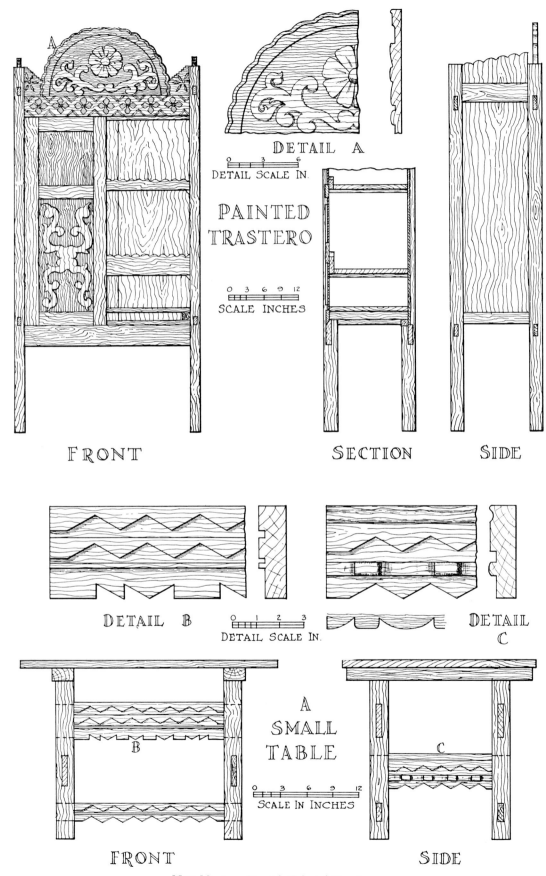

DETAIL A

DETAIL SCALE IN.
0   3   6

PAINTED
TRASTERO

0   3   6   9   12
SCALE INCHES

FRONT   SECTION   SIDE

DETAIL B   0   1   2   3   DETAIL
                DETAIL SCALE IN.   C

A
SMALL
TABLE

0   3   6   9   12
SCALE IN INCHES

FRONT   SIDE

New Mexican Spanish-Colonial Furniture

Plate 45

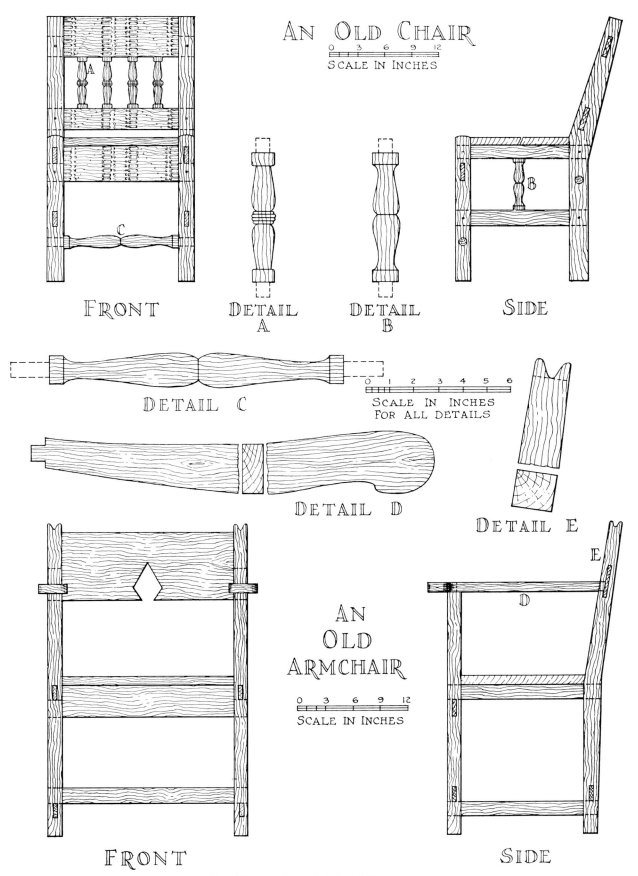

AN OLD CHAIR

SCALE IN INCHES

FRONT

DETAIL A

DETAIL B

SIDE

DETAIL C

SCALE IN INCHES
FOR ALL DETAILS

DETAIL D

DETAIL E

AN
OLD
ARMCHAIR

SCALE IN INCHES

FRONT

SIDE

New Mexican Spanish-Colonial Furniture

Plate 46

FRONT   END

A PAINTED CHEST

0   1   2
SCALE IN FEET

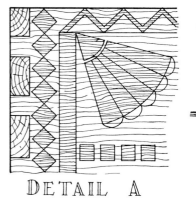

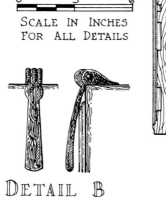

0   3   6
SCALE IN INCHES
FOR ALL DETAILS

DETAIL A   DETAIL C

DETAIL B

AN OLD CHEST

0   1   2
SCALE IN FEET

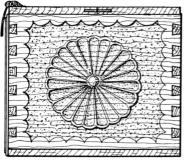

FRONT   END

New Mexican Spanish-Colonial Furniture

Plate 47

General View

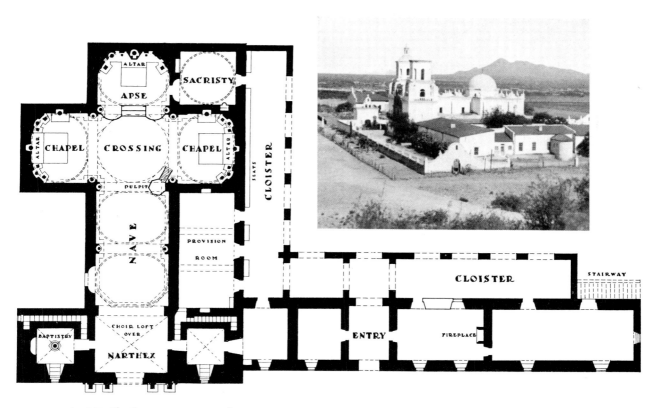

MISSION SAN XAVIER DEL BAC

NEAR TUCSON ARIZONA

BASED UPON SURVEYS BY PRENTICE DUELL

SCALE IN FEET

Mission San Xavier del Bac, near Tucson, Arizona
(Photos. by Putnam Studios)

Plate 48

Facade. Mission San Xavier del Bac, near Tucson, Arizona
(Photo. by Putnam Studios)

Plate 49

Mission San Xavier del Bac, near Tucson, Arizona. — Side of Church

(*Photo. by Putnam Studios*)

Plate 50

Mission San Xavier del Bac, near Tucson, Arizona. — Interior looking toward Altar
(*Photo. by Putnam Studios*)

Plate 51

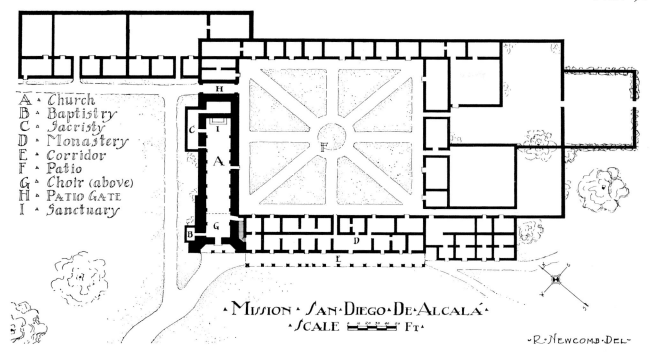

A ⸱ Church
B ⸱ Baptistry
C ⸱ Sacristy
D ⸱ Monastery
E ⸱ Corridor
F ⸱ Patio
G ⸱ Choir (above)
H ⸱ Patio Gate
I ⸱ Sanctuary

⸱Mission⸱San⸱Diego⸱De⸱Alcalá⸱
⸱Scale ▭▭▭ Ft⸱

⸱R⸱Newcomb⸱Del⸱

Plan

General View — Restored   (*Photo. by H. Pascal Webb*)

Mission San Diego Alcalá, near San Diego, California. (Restoration by J. Marshall Miller, Architect)

Plate 52

Campanario from Patio Arcade

Campanario Restored

Mission San Diego de Alcalá, near San Diego, California. (Restoration by J. Marshall Miller, Architect)

(Photos. by Lester B. Ford)

Plate 53

Bell

Side Doorway of Church

Detail of Main Doorway   (Photos. by Lester B. Ford)   *Main Doorway of Church*

Mission San Diego de Alcalá, near San Diego, California. (Restoration by J. Marshall Miller, Architect)

Plate 54

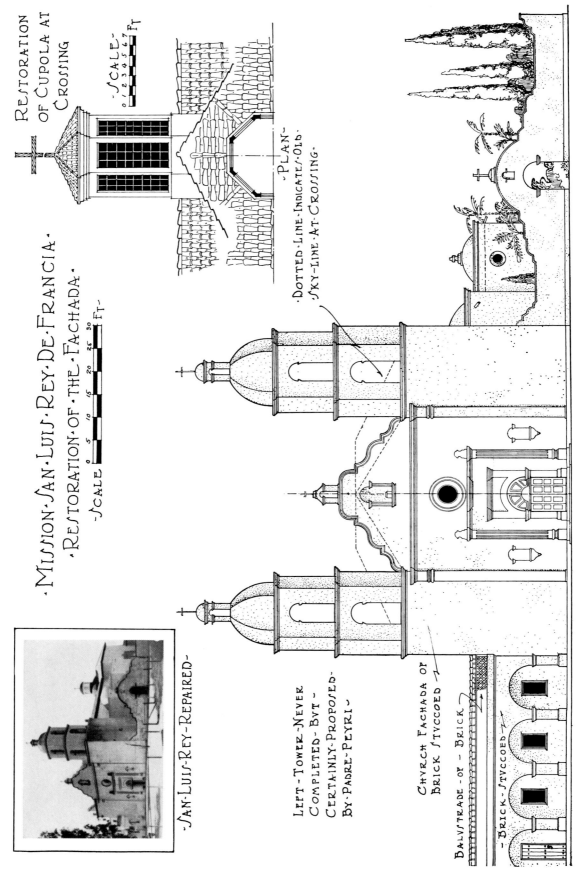

RESTORATION OF CUPOLA AT CROSSING

SCALE
0 1 2 3 4 5 6 7 FT

·PLAN·
·DOTTED·LINE·INDICATES·OLD·
·SKY·LINE·AT·CROSSING·

·MISSION·SAN·LUIS·REY·DE·FRANCIA·
·RESTORATION·OF·THE·FACHADA·
·SCALE·

SCALE
0 5 10 15 20 25 30 FT

·SAN·LUIS·REY·REPAIRED·

LEFT·TOWER·NEVER·
COMPLETED·BVT·
CERTAINLY·PROPOSED·
BY·PADRE·PEYRI·

CHVRCH·FACHADA·OF·
BRICK·STVCCOED·

BALVSTRADE·OF·BRICK·

·BRICK·STVCCOED·

Mission San Luis Rey de Francia, California. — Restoration of the Facade

Plate 55

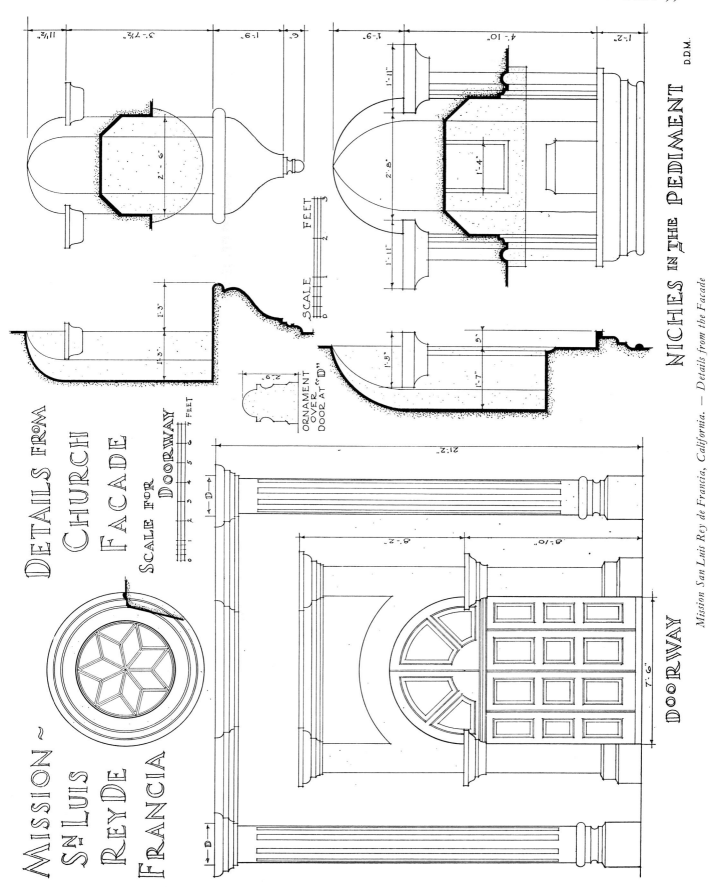

NICHES IN THE PEDIMENT

D.D.M.

SCALE FEET

ORNAMENT OVER DOOR AT "D"

DETAILS FROM CHURCH FACADE

SCALE FOR DOORWAY

FEET

MISSION ~ SⁿLUIS REY DE FRANCIA

DOORWAY

Mission San Luis Rey de Francia, California. — Details from the Facade

Plate 56

Mortuary Chapel before Restoration

General View before Restoration

The Patio before Restoration

Mission San Luis Rey de Francia

Plate 57

·Stucco·on·Brick·

·Side·Doorway·of·Church·
·Mission·San·Luis·Rey·de·Francia·
·Scale· 0 1 2 3 4 5 Ft ·

Mission San Luis Rey de Francia, California. — Side Doorway of Church

Plate 58

Interior of Church

Pulpit and Side Altar

Pilasters at Crossing

Mission San Luis Rey de Francia, California

(Courtesy J. B. Lippincott Co. Photos. by Putnam Studios)

Plate 59

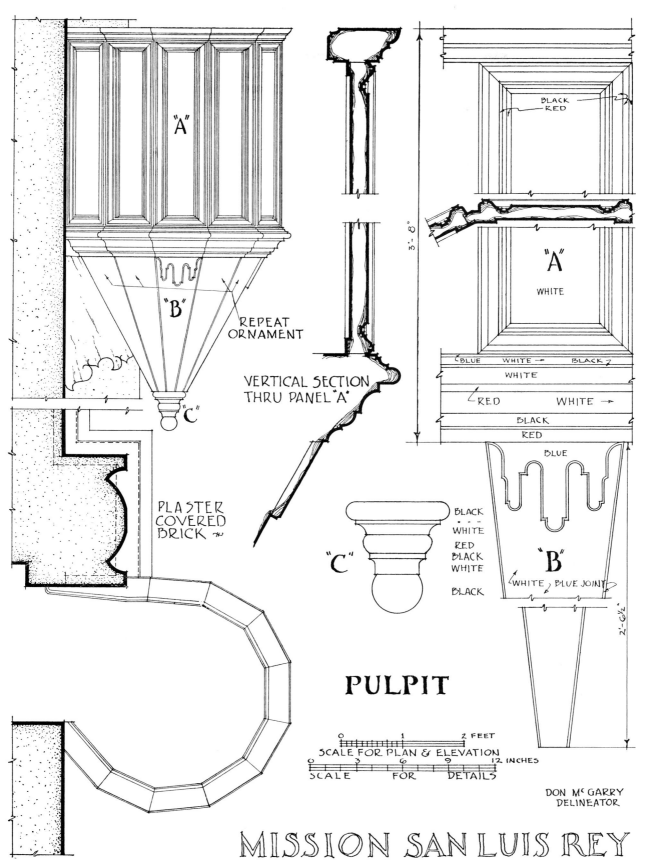

"A"

"B"

REPEAT
ORNAMENT

VERTICAL SECTION
THRU PANEL "A"

PLASTER
COVERED
BRICK

"C"

BLACK
RED

"A"

WHITE

BLUE   WHITE →   BLACK
WHITE
RED   WHITE →
BLACK
RED

BLUE

"B"

WHITE   BLUE JOINT

3'- 8"

2'- 6½"

"C"

BLACK
WHITE
RED
BLACK
WHITE

BLACK

PULPIT

0   1   2 FEET
SCALE FOR PLAN & ELEVATION

0   3   6   9   12 INCHES
SCALE   FOR   DETAILS

DON M°GARRY
DELINEATOR

MISSION SAN LUIS REY

Mission San Luis Rey de Francia. — Details of Pulpit

Plate 60

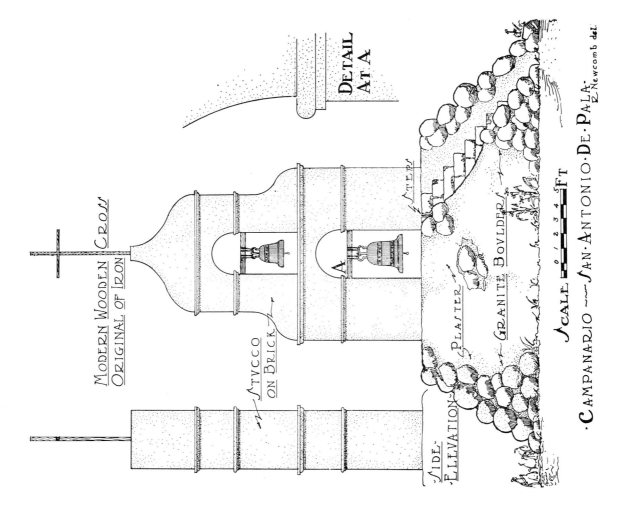

MODERN WOODEN CROSS
ORIGINAL OF IRON

STVCCO
ON BRICK

DETAIL
AT A

A

STEPS

PLASTER

GRANITE BOVLDERS

SIDE-ELEVATION

SCALE 0 1 2 3 4 5 FT

·CAMPANARIO ~ SAN·ANTONIO·DE·PALA·
R. Newcomb del.

Asistencia de San Antonio de Pala, California, — Campanario
(Photographs by Putnam Studios)

Plate 61

Mission San Juan Capistrano, California
From a painting by Behyr

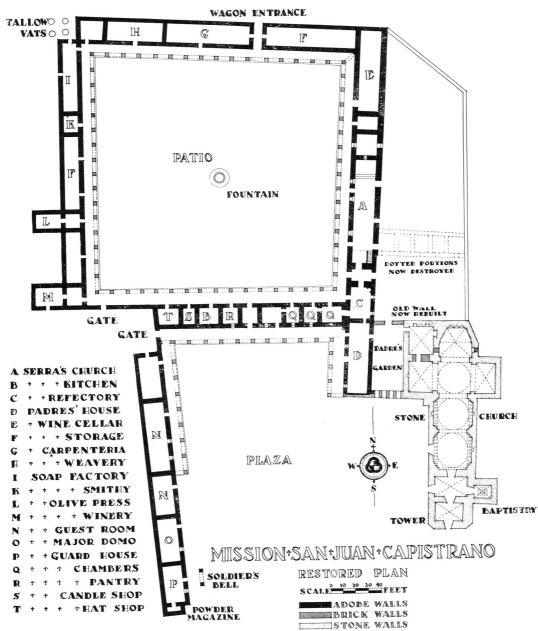

A SERRA'S CHURCH
B + + + KITCHEN
C + + REFECTORY
D PADRES' HOUSE
E + WINE CELLAR
F + + + STORAGE
G + CARPENTERIA
H + + + WEAVERY
I SOAP FACTORY
K + + + + SMITHY
L + OLIVE PRESS
M + + + + WINERY
N + + GUEST ROOM
O + + MAJOR DOMO
P + + GUARD HOUSE
Q + + + + CHAMBERS
R + + + + PANTRY
S + + CANDLE SHOP
T + + + HAT SHOP

MISSION·SAN·JUAN·CAPISTRANO
RESTORED PLAN
SCALE 0 10 20 30 40 FEET
ADOBE WALLS
BRICK WALLS
STONE WALLS

Plan

Plate 62

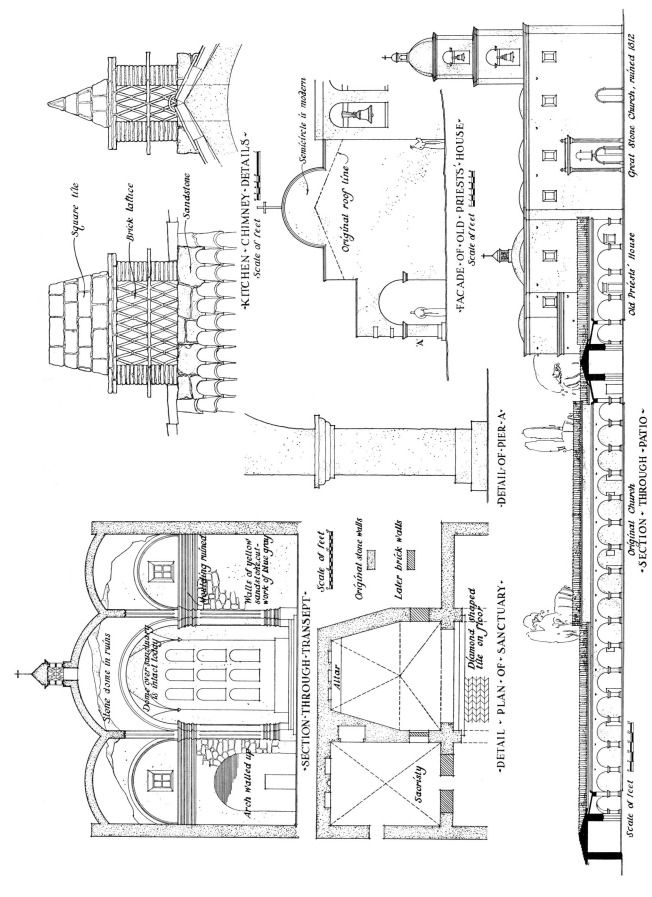

Square tile

Brick lattice

Sandstone

·KITCHEN·CHIMNEY·DETAILS·
Scale of feet

Semicircle is modern

Original roof line

·FACADE·OF·OLD·PRIESTS'·HOUSE·
Scale of feet

A

·DETAIL·OF·PIER·A·

Stone dome in ruins

Walls of yellow sandstone cut-work of blue gray

Vaulting ruined

Dome over sanctuary is intact today

Arch walled up

·SECTION·THROUGH·TRANSEPT·

Scale of feet

Original stone walls

Later brick walls

Altar

Sacristy

Diamond shaped tile on floor

·DETAIL·PLAN·OF·SANCTUARY·

Great Stone Church, ruined 1812

Old Priests' House

Original Church

·SECTION·THROUGH·PATIO·

Scale of feet

Mission San Juan Capistrano, California

Plate 63

(Courtesy J. B. Lippincott Co. Photo. by Putnam Studios.)

Mission San Juan Capistrano, California. — Ruined Sanctuary

Plate 64

Broken Arches in the Patio   (Courtesy J. B. Lippincott Co.)

Mission San Juan Capistrano, California

Front Arcade of the Mission

Plate 65

Campanario and Buttresses

West End Showing Curved Gable

Mission San Gabriel Arcángel, near Los Ángeles, California

(Photos. by Putnam Studios)

Plate 66

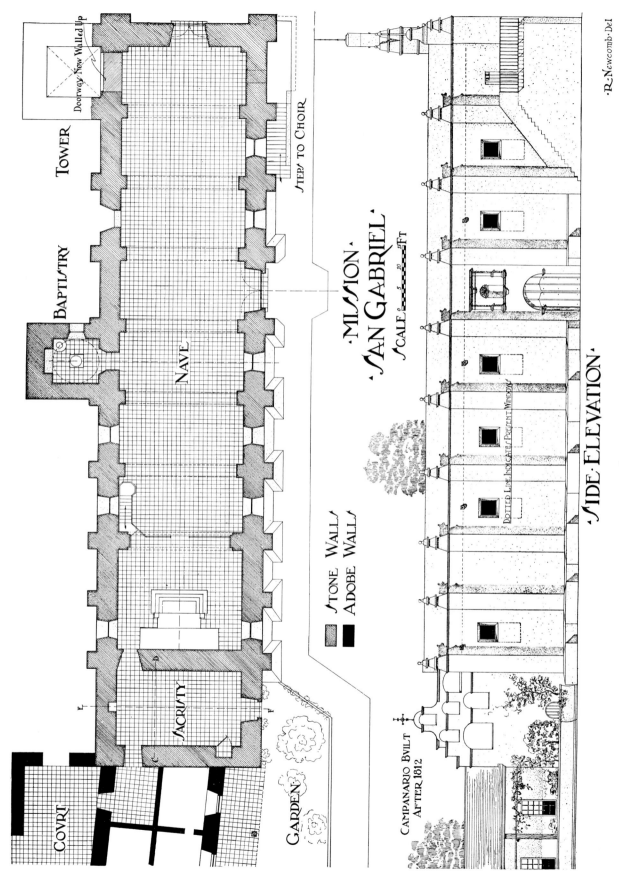

TOWER

BAPTISTRY

NAVE

SACRISTY

COURT

GARDEN

Doorway Now Walled Up

STEPS TO CHOIR

·MISSION·
·SAN GABRIEL·
SCALE 0 5 10 FT

STONE WALLS
ADOBE WALLS

·SIDE·ELEVATION·

CAMPANARIO BUILT
AFTER 1812

DOTTED LINE INDICATES PRESENT WINDOW

·R·Newcomb·Del

Mission San Gabriel Arcángel, near Los Ángeles, California. — Plan and Side Elevation

Plate 67

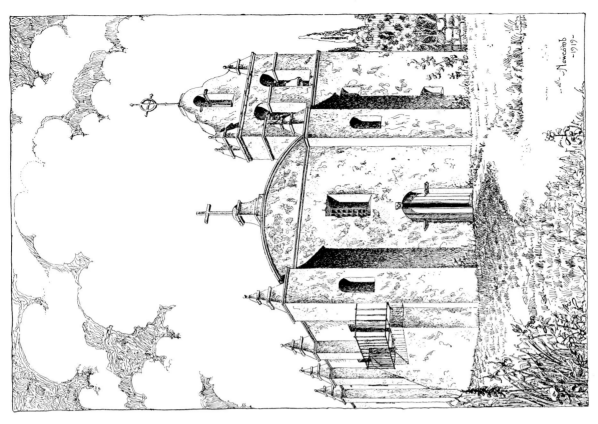

Conjectural Restoration of the Mission Church

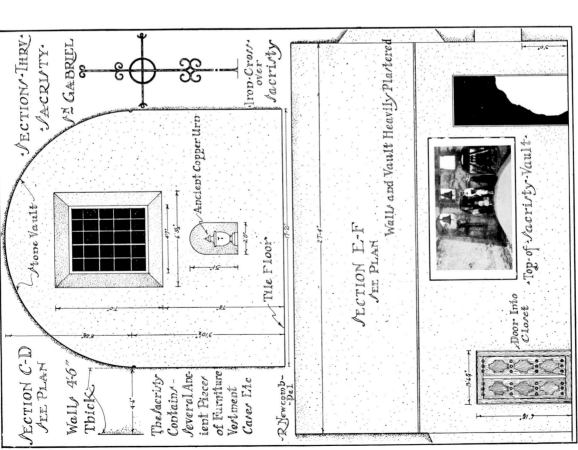

·SECTION·THRU·
·SACRISTY·
·S. GABRIEL·

·SECTION· C-D·
·SEE PLAN·

Walls 4'-6"
Thick

·Stone Vault·

The Sacristy
Contains
Several An-
cient Pieces
of Furniture
Vestment
Cases Etc

·Ancient Copper Urn·

·Tile Floor·

·R.Newcomb·
-Del-

·Iron·Cross·
over·
·Sacristy·

·SECTION E-F·
·SEE PLAN·

Walls and Vault Heavily Plastered

·Door Into
Closet·   ·Top of· Sacristy·Vault·

Sections through Sacristy (see Plan)

Mission San Gabriel Arcángel, near Los Angeles, California

Plate 68

Mission San Gabriel Arcángel, near Los Ángeles, California. — Side Doorway   (*Photo. by Putnam Studios*)

Plate 69

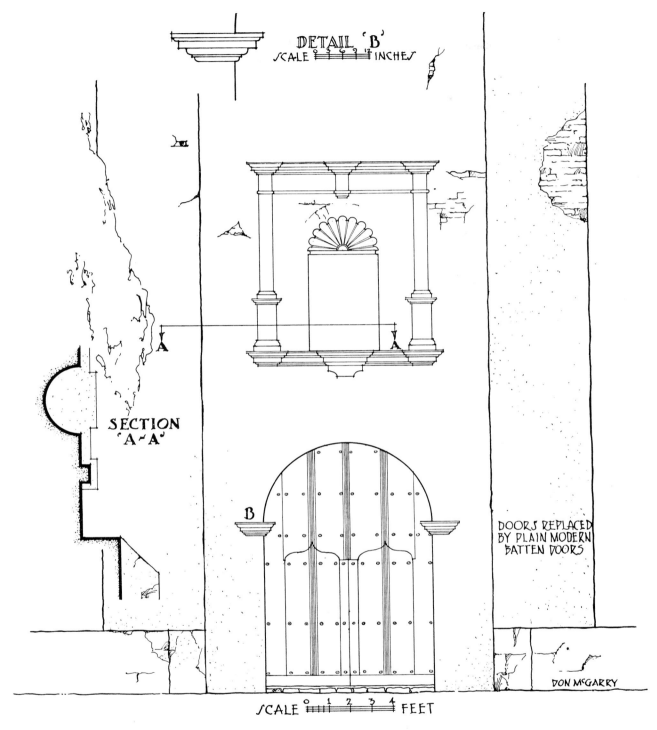

DETAIL 'B'
SCALE INCHES

SECTION 'A-A'

A   A

B

DOORS REPLACED
BY PLAIN MODERN
BATTEN DOORS

DON McGARRY

SCALE 0 1 2 3 4 FEET

DOORWAY
MISSION ~ SAN GABRIEL

Mission San Gabriel Arcángel, near Los Ángeles, California. — Side Doorway

Plate 70

General View

(Keystone Photo)

Side Elevation

Corner Detail

Old Mill of Mission San Gabriel Arcángel, near Pasadena, California

(Photos. by Putnam Studios)

(The wooden porches, not original have now been removed)

Plate 71

PLAN
SCALE FEET

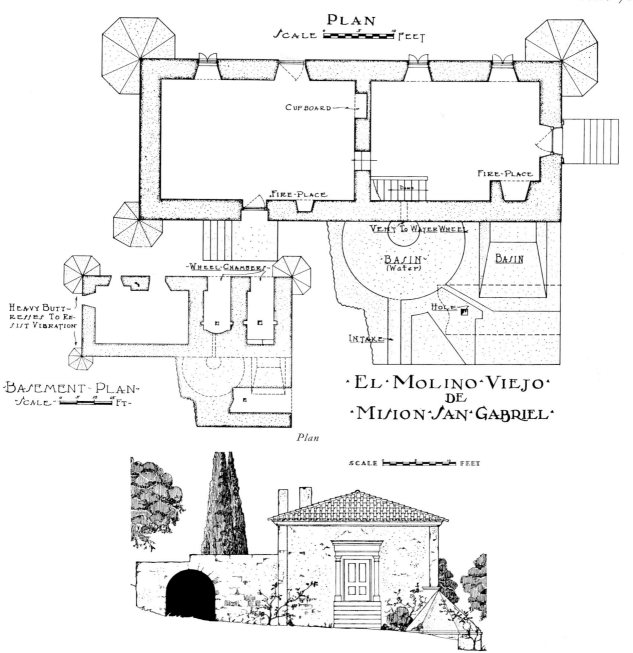

CUPBOARD

FIRE-PLACE

FIRE-PLACE

VENT TO WATER WHEEL

BASIN
(Water)

BASIN

HOLE

INTAKE

WHEEL-CHAMBERS

HEAVY BUTT-
RESSES TO RE-
SIST VIBRATION

BASEMENT PLAN
SCALE 0 5 10 15 FT

·EL·MOLINO·VIEJO·
DE
·MISION·SAN·GABRIEL·

Plan

SCALE FEET

End Elevation

SCALE FEET

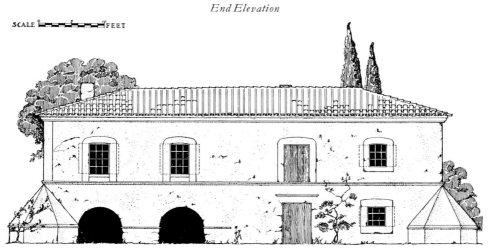

Side Elevation   *(Courtesy J. B. Lippincott Co.)*

Old Mill of Mission San Gabriel Arcángel, near Pasadena, California

Plate 72

Fountain and Mission House

Front Corridor of the Mission House
Mission San Fernando Rey de España, California

Plate 73

Old Dining Room

Corner of Mission House Showing Belfry   *Mission San Fernando Rey de España, California*
(Photos. by Author)

Plate 74

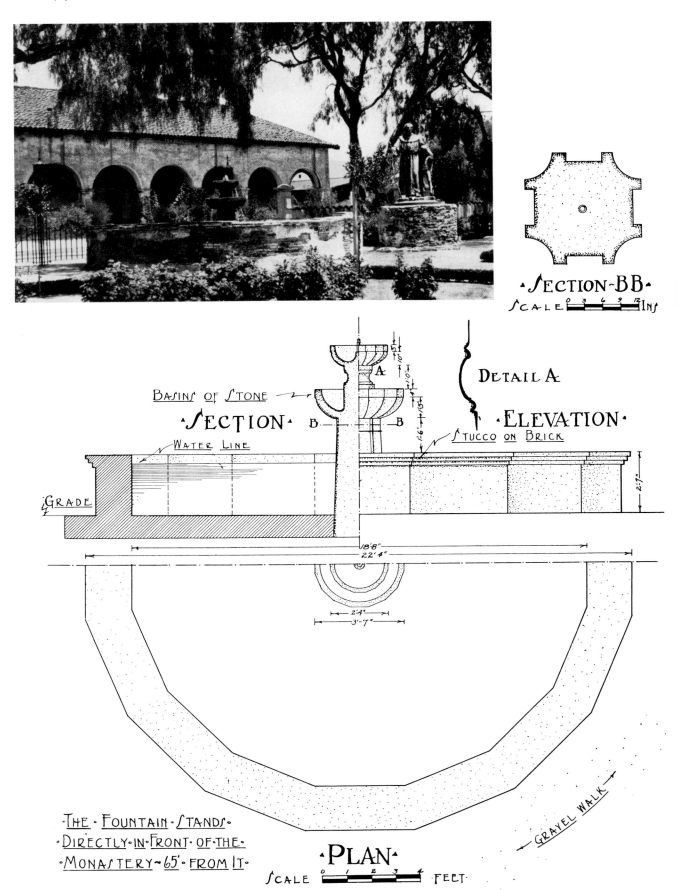

SECTION-BB·
SCALE

BASINS OF STONE

DETAIL A

·SECTION· B — B

·ELEVATION·

STUCCO ON BRICK

WATER LINE

GRADE

18'8"

22'4"

2'4"

3'-7"

GRAVEL WALK

THE·FOUNTAIN·STANDS·
·DIRECTLY·IN·FRONT·OF·THE·
·MONASTERY~65'·FROM·IT·

·PLAN·

SCALE   0   1   2   3   4   FEET·

Mission San Fernando Rey de España, California. — Fountain

Plate 75

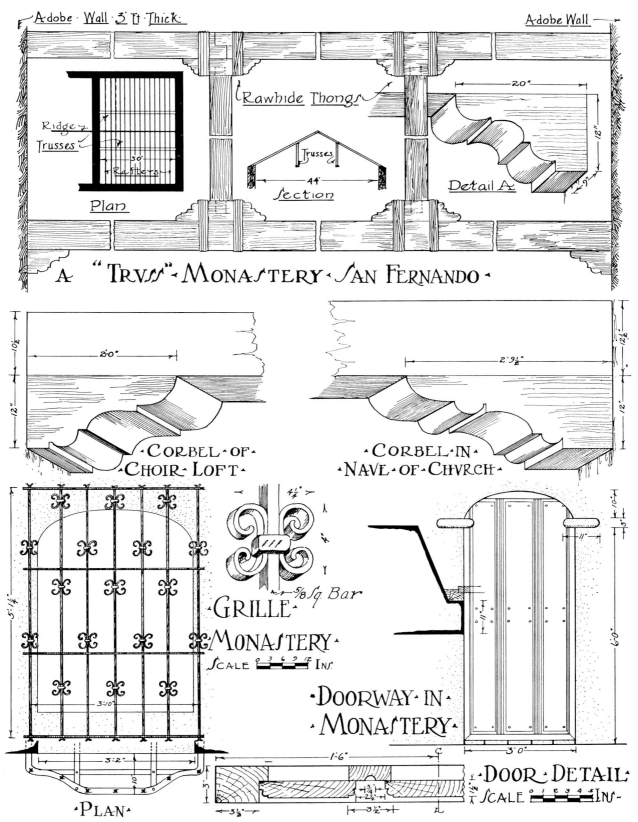

Adobe · Wall · 3 · Ft · Thick·

Adobe Wall

Rawhide Thongs

Ridge
Trusses

Rafters

30'

Trusses

44'

Plan

Section

20"

12"

Detail A

A · "TRUSS"· MONASTERY · SAN FERNANDO ·

CORBEL · OF·
CHOIR · LOFT

10½'

12"

2'0"

CORBEL · IN·
·NAVE · OF · CHVRCH·

12½'

2'9½"

12"

GRILLE
· MONASTERY ·
SCALE 0 3 6 9 12 INS.

4½"

⅝ Sq Bar

·DOORWAY· IN ·
MONASTERY ·

3·10½'

3'0"

PLAN·

3'2"

10"

DOOR · DETAIL·
SCALE 0 1 2 3 4 5 INS

1'6"

3"

3½"

3½"

2½"

·Mission San Fernando Rey de España, California. — Details·

Plate 76

General View   *(Photo. by Putnam Studios)*

In the Belfry   *(Photo. by Author)*

Mission San Buenaventura, Ventura, California

Plate 77

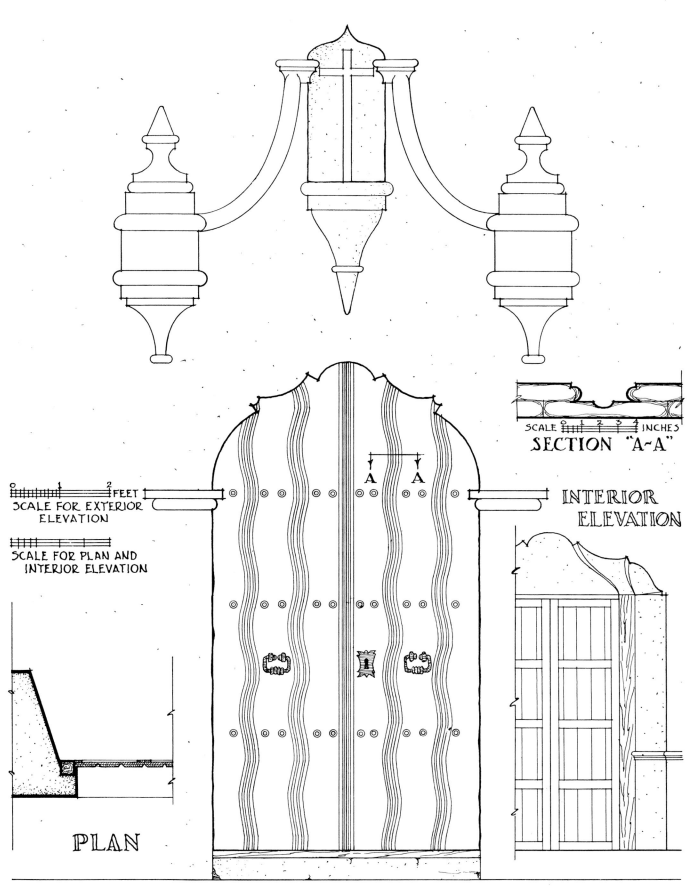

SCALE 0 1 2 3 4 INCHES
SECTION "A~A"

SCALE FOR EXTERIOR
ELEVATION

SCALE FOR PLAN AND
INTERIOR ELEVATION

0 1 2 FEET

A   A

INTERIOR ELEVATION

PLAN

Mission San Buenaventura, Ventura, California. — Side Door

Plate 78

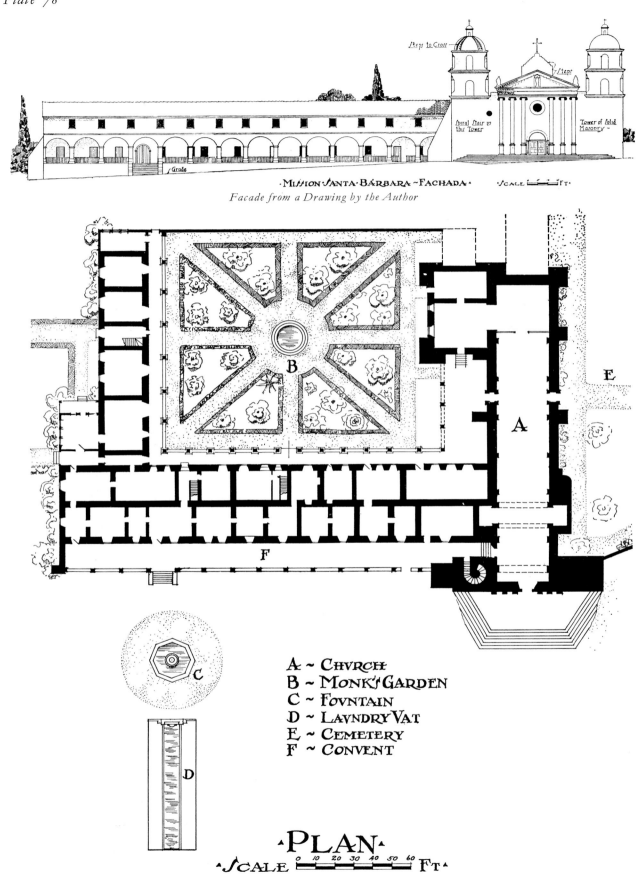

Steps to Cross

Steps

·MISSION·SANTA·BÁRBARA·~FACHADA·   ·SCALE   FT·

Spiral Stair to this Tower

Tower of Solid Masonry ~

Grade

Facade from a Drawing by the Author

E

A

B

F

C

D

A ~ CHVRCH
B ~ MONK'S GARDEN
C ~ FOVNTAIN
D ~ LAVNDRY VAT
E ~ CEMETERY
F ~ CONVENT

·PLAN·
·SCALE   0 10 20 30 40 50 60   FT·

Plan

Santa Bárbara, Santa Bárbara, California

Plate 79

General View

Church from the Plaza

Interior of Church   (*Photo. by Putnam Studios*)

Mission Santa Bárbara, Santa Bárbara, California.

Plate 80

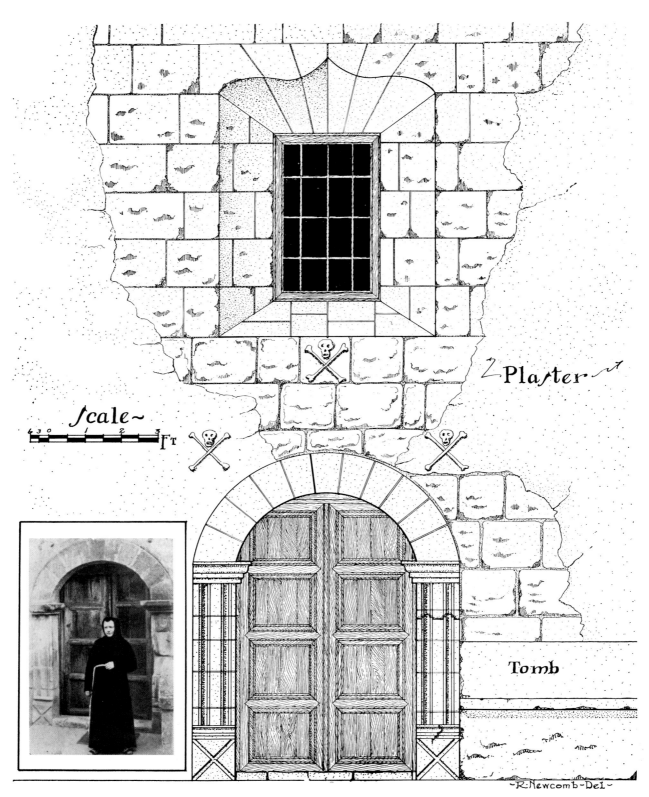

Scale~

Plaster

Tomb

~R·Newcomb·Del~

Mission Santa Bárbara, Santa Bárbara, California. — Detail of Doorway from Church into Cemetery

Plate 81

Front View   *(Photo. by Putnam Studios)*

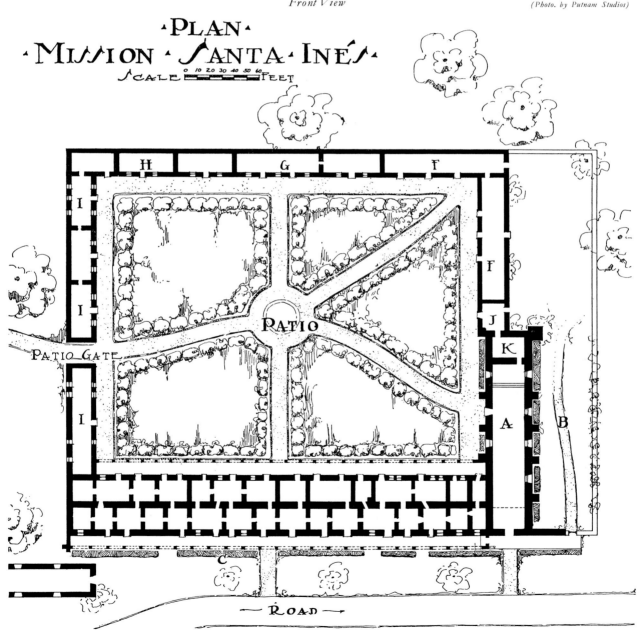

Plan
Mission Santa Inés, Solvang, California

Plate 82

Front Elevation

Detail of the Cloister. — Mission Santa Inés, Solvang, California
(Courtesy J. B. Lippincott Co. Photo. by Author)

Plate 83

The Church as It Looked Years Ago

(Photo. by Putnam Studios)

(Keystone Photo)

The Church before Recent Restoration of the Roof

Mission San Carlos de Borromeo (Carmel), Carmel, California

Plate 84

Stair Detail

(Photo. by Author)

Belfry and Stairway

(Photo. by Putnam Studios)

Mission San Carlos de Borromeo (Carmel), Carmel, California

(Courtesy J. B. Lippincott Co.)

Plate 85

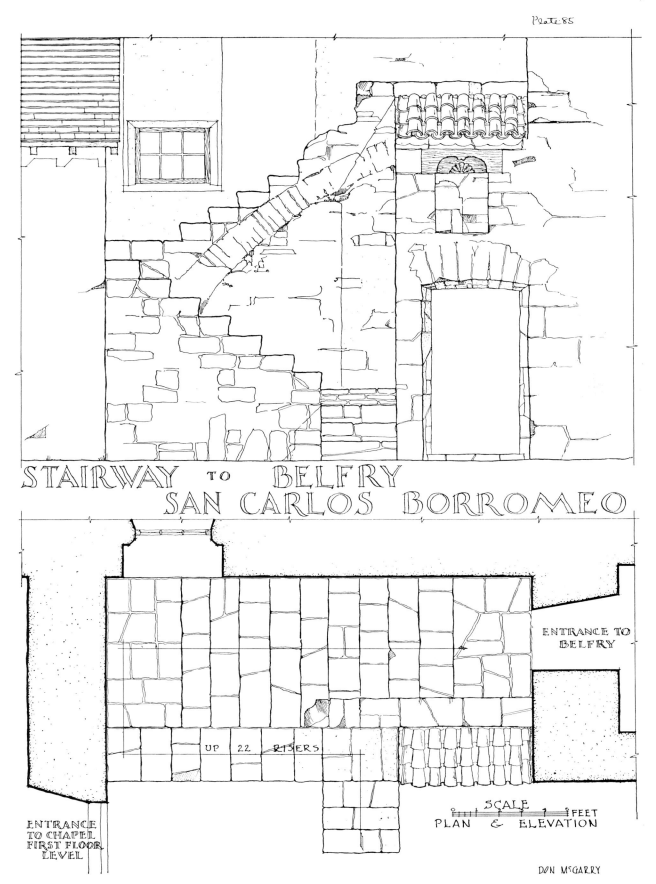

Plate 85

STAIRWAY TO BELFRY
SAN CARLOS BORROMEO

ENTRANCE TO BELFRY

UP 22 RISERS

ENTRANCE TO CHAPEL FIRST FLOOR LEVEL

SCALE FEET
PLAN & ELEVATION

DON M?GARRY

Mission San Carlos de Borromeo (Carmel), Carmel, California. — Stairway to Belfry

Plate 86

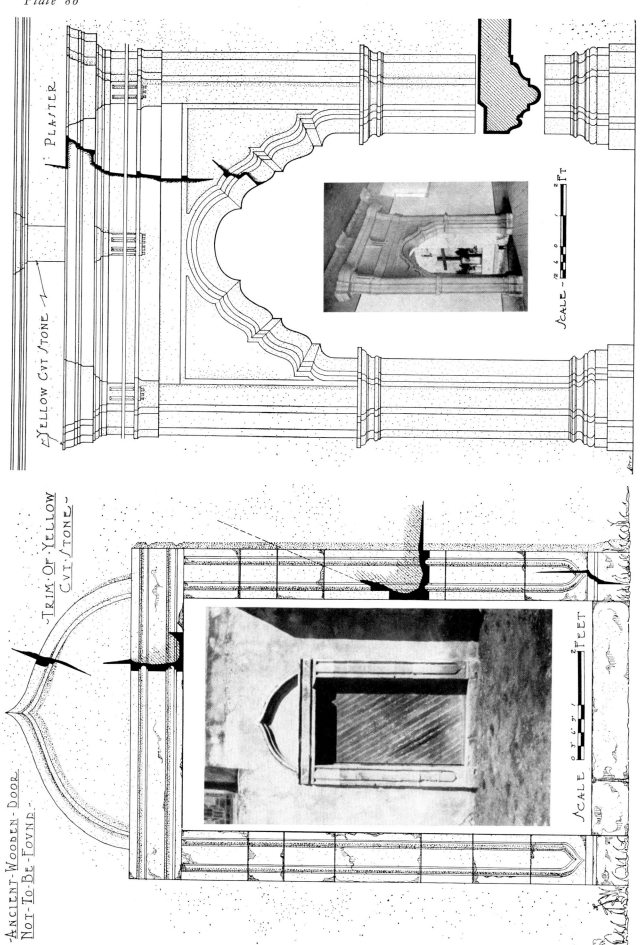

PLASTER

YELLOW CVT STONE

SCALE ~ 12 6 0 1 2 FT

Doorway into Chapel (Interior)

ANCIENT·WOODEN·DOOR·
NOT·TO·BE·FOVND·

TRIM·OF·YELLOW·
CVT·STONE·

SCALE ~ 0 3 6 9 1 2 FEET

Doorway on Side of Church

Mission San Carlos de Borromeo (Carmel), Carmel, California

Plate 87

Curved Gable on Church Facade

(Photos. by Slevin)

Main Doorway

(Courtesy J. B. Lippincott Co.)

Facade of the Church   *(Photo. by Putnam Studios)*

The Old "Royal Chapel", Monterey, California (now San Carlos Church)

Plate 88

CAPILLA REAL DE SAN CARLOS
~ MONTEREY ~

SCALE IN FEET

The Old "Royal Chapel", Monterey, California. — Facade

Plate 89

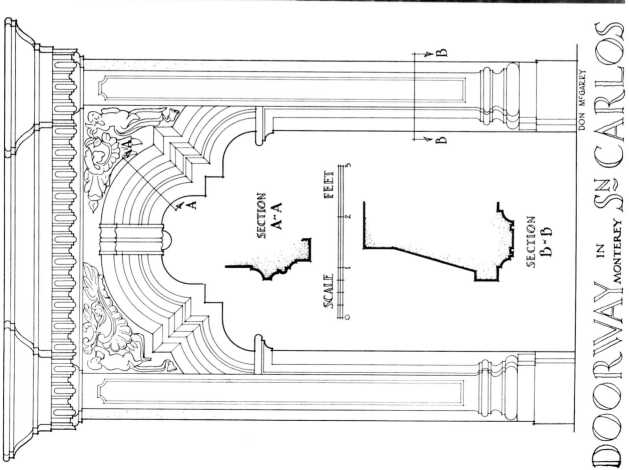

(Photo. by Author)

DOORWAY IN SN CARLOS
MONTEREY

DON McGARRY

SECTION A~A

SECTION B~B

SCALE
FEET

0   1   2   3

The Old "Royal Chapel", Monterey, California. — Transept Doorway

Plate 90

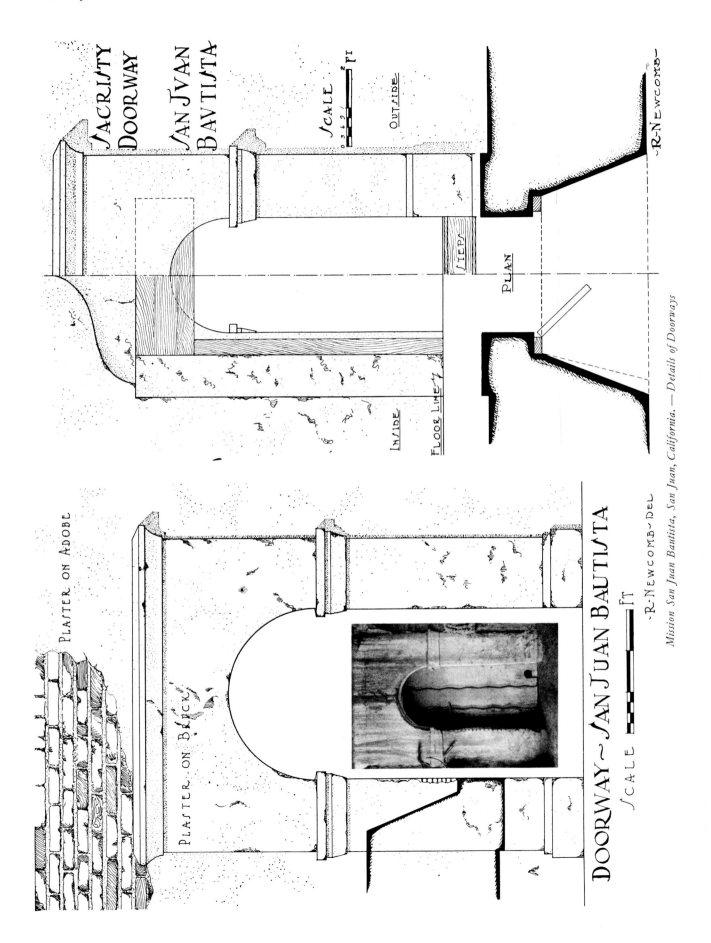

SACRISTY DOORWAY SAN JUAN BAUTISTA

SCALE
0 3 6 9   2 FT

OUTSIDE

INSIDE

FLOOR LINE

VIEW

PLAN

R·Newcomb

PLASTER ON ADOBE

PLASTER ON BRICK

DOORWAY ~ SAN JUAN BAUTISTA

SCALE   FT

R·Newcomb·Del

Mission San Juan Bautista, San Juan, California. — Details of Doorways

Plate 91

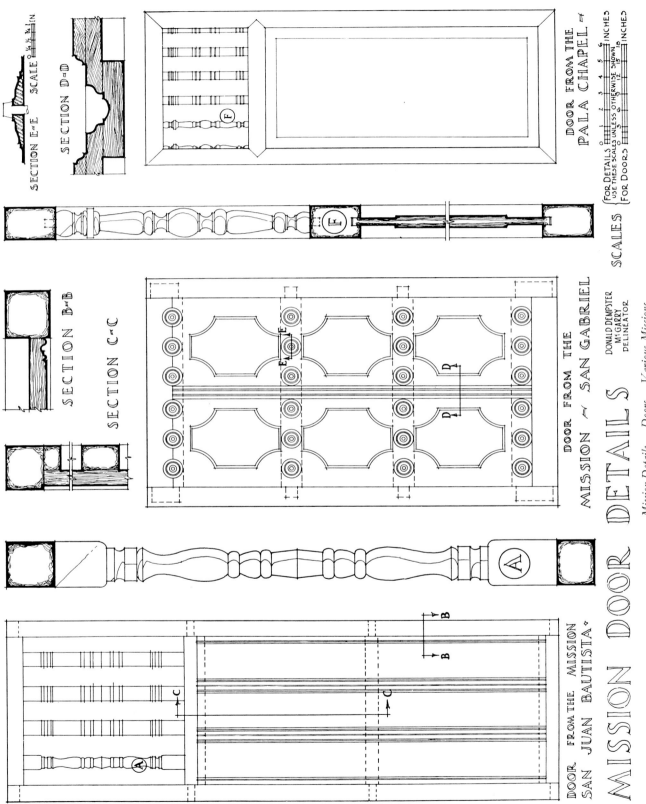

SECTION E-E   SCALE ¼ ¼ ¾ IN

SECTION D-D

SECTION B-B

SECTION C-C

DOOR FROM THE
PALA CHAPEL

DOOR FROM THE
MISSION ~ SAN GABRIEL

DOOR FROM THE MISSION
SAN JUAN BAUTISTA·

SCALES

(FOR DETAILS
USE THESE SCALES UNLESS OTHERWISE SHOWN
(FOR DOORS

DONALD DEMPSTER
McGARRY
DELINEATOR

MISSION DOOR DETAILS

Mission Details — Doors — Various Missions

Plate 92

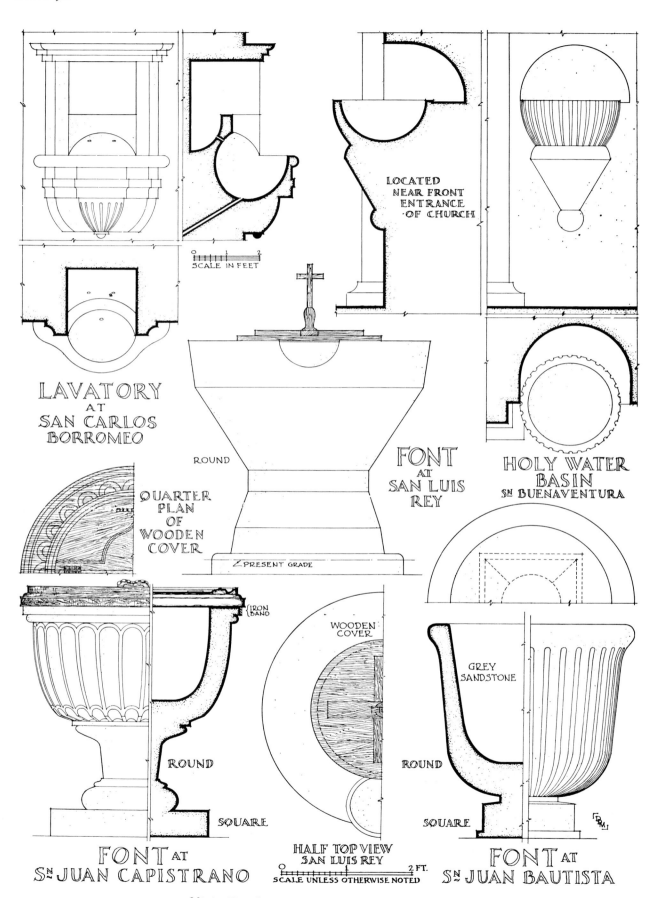

LAVATORY
AT
SAN CARLOS
BORROMEO

SCALE IN FEET

LOCATED
NEAR FRONT
ENTRANCE
·OF·CHURCH

ROUND

QUARTER
PLAN
OF
WOODEN
COVER

FONT
AT
SAN LUIS
REY

PRESENT GRADE

HOLY WATER
BASIN
Sⁿ BUENAVENTURA

IRON
BAND

ROUND

SQUARE

WOODEN
COVER

GREY
SANDSTONE

ROUND

SQUARE

FONT AT
Sⁿ JUAN CAPISTRANO

HALF TOP VIEW
SAN LUIS REY
SCALE UNLESS OTHERWISE NOTED

2 FT.

FONT AT
Sⁿ JUAN BAUTISTA

Mission Details — Fonts and Basins — Various Missions

Plate 93

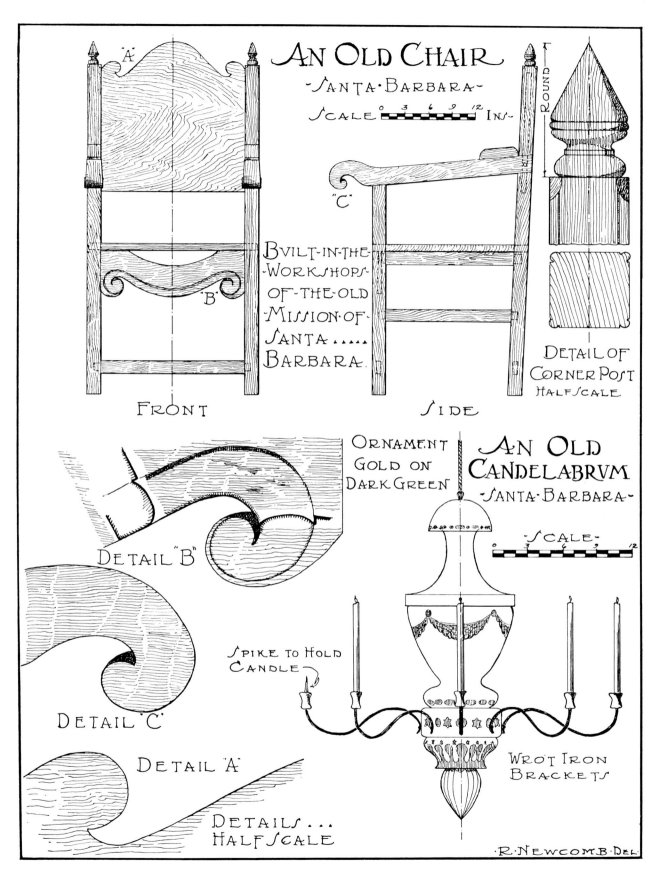

AN OLD CHAIR
-Santa·Barbara-
Scale 0 3 6 9 12 Ins-

Round

"C"

Bvilt·in·the·Workshops·of·the·old·Mission·of·Santa.....Barbara·

Detail of Corner Post Half Scale

FRONT

SIDE

Detail "B"

Ornament Gold on Dark Green

AN OLD CANDELABRVM
-Santa·Barbara-

Scale 0 3 6 9 12

Detail "C"

Spike to Hold Candle

Detail "A"

Details... Half Scale

Wro't Iron Brackets

·R·Newcomb·Del·

Mission Details — Furniture

Plate 94

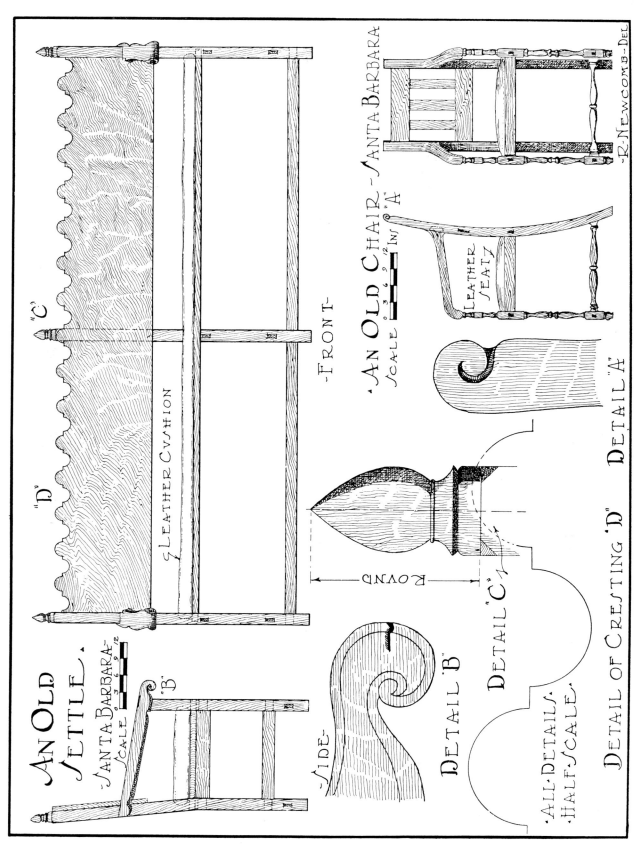

An Old Settle.
~Santa Barbara~
Scale

"B"

"C"   "D"

Leather Cushion

~Side~   ~Front~

Detail "B"

Detail "C"

Round

An Old Chair ~Santa Barbara~
Scale   Ins.   "A"

Leather Seats

Detail "A"

Detail of Cresting "D"

·All·Details·
·Half·Scale·

-R·Newcomb-Del-

Plate 95

Exterior

Interior   *(Photos. by Hoit)*

Congregational Church, Coral Gables, Florida. Kiehnel and Elliott, Architects

Plate 96

Outdoor Pulpit in Patio

Entrance　　(Photos. by Hoit)

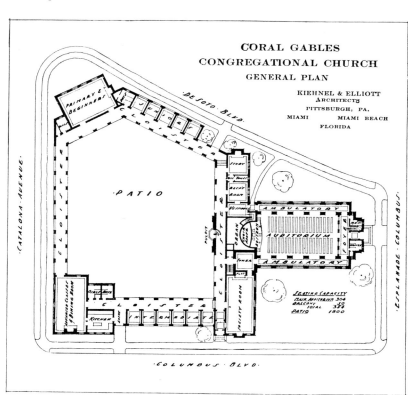

Plan

Congregational Church, Coral Gables, Florida. Kiehnel and Elliott, Architects

Plate 97

School, Coral Gables, Florida. Kiehnel and Elliott, Architects

Bank of Coral Gables, Florida. Kiehnel and Elliott, Architects
(Photos. by Fishbaugh)

Plate 98

Holy Trinity Church, West Palm Beach, Florida. Harvey and Clark, Architects

Residence of Robert S. Weed, Miami Beach, Florida. Robert S. Weed, Architect   (Photo. by Van Dyke)

Plate 99

Water Tower, Alhambra Circle

Street Lamp, Ponce de Leon Plaza

Lagoon, Casino and Bridge
Landscape Details, Coral Gables, Florida

(Photos. by Fishbaugh)

Plate 100

Missouri-Kansas-Texas Railway Station, San Antonio, Texas, Frederick Sterner, Architect

Plate 101

Meadows Hotel, Las Vegas, New Mexico. (In the Texan Style)

Hotel Paisani, Marfa, Texas. — Interior, Trost and Trost, Architects

Plate 102

General View

Entrance Detail

Residence of Charles W. Oliver, Houston, Texas. Charles W. Oliver, Architect

Plate 103

Front Facade

Front Porch   (Photos. by Harvey Patterson)

Hacienda de la Tordilla, near San Antonio, Texas. Harvey P. Smith, Architect

Plate 104

Living Room

Dining Room (Photos. by Harvey Patterson)

Hacienda de la Tordilla, near San Antonio, Texas. Harvey P. Smith, Architect

Plate 105

General View of Front

The Portales

Federal Building, Santa Fé, New Mexico. James A. Wetmore, Supervising Architect, Treasury Department

Plate 106

General View from Plaza

Detail of Laguna Elevation   *(Photos. by School of American Research)*

Museum of New Mexico, Santa Fé, New Mexico. I. H. Rapp, W. M. Rapp and A. C. Hendrickson, Architects

Plate 107

Museum of New Mexico, Santa Fé, New Mexico. — Patio. I. H. Rapp, W. M. Rapp and A. C. Hendrickson, Architects

Building for the Santa Fé Water and Light Company, Santa Fé, New Mexico. I. H. Rapp, W. M. Rapp and A. C. Hendrickson, Architects
(Photos. by School of American Resarch)

Plate 108

Residence of Carlos Vierra, Santa Fé, New Mexico. Carlos Vierra, Architect

Library Wing, Palace of the Governors', Santa Fé, New Mexico

(Photos. Courtesy of J. B. Lippincott Co.)

Residence of Milton Helmick, Albuquerque, New Mexico. E. C. Morgan Architect

Plate 109

Laboratory of Anthropology, Santa Fé, New Mexico. John Gaw Meem, Architect

Memorial Chapel for Mrs. F. M. P. Taylor, Colorado Springs, Colorado. John Gaw Meem, Architect

Plate 110

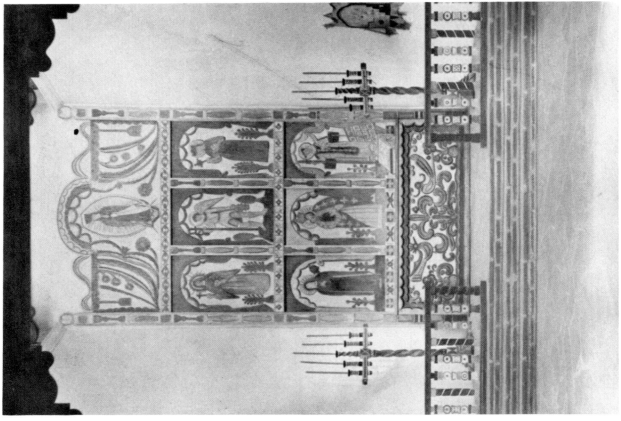

Altar

Doorway

Memorial Chapel for Mrs. F. M. P. Taylor, Colorado Springs, Colorado. John Gaw Meem, Architect

Plate III

Saint Augustine Cathedral, Tucson, Arizona. Henry O. Jaastad, Architect

Plate 112

Saint Thomas Roman Catholic Church, Ojai, California. Mead and Requa, Architects

Post Office Tower and Ojai State Bank, Ojai, California. Requa and Jackson, Architects

Plate 113

Unitarian Church, Santa Bárbara, California. E. K. Lockard, Architect

Court, Unitarian Church, Santa Bárbara, California
(Photos. by F. G. Anderson)

Plate 114

Court of the Birds

(Photos by A. E. Field)
Spanish Art Gallery

Glenwood Mission Inn, Riverside, California. Arthur B. Benton, Architect

Plate 115

Oldest Dated Bell in Christendom

Glenwood Mission Inn, Riverside, California. Arthur B. Benton, Architect

Carmel Tower

Plate 116

Beverly Hills Hotel, Beverly Hills, California   (Photo. by Don. Milton)

(Photo. by F. G. Andersen)

Santa Bárbara County Court House, Santa Bárbara, California. William Mooser Company, Architect

Plate 117

Entrance Drive

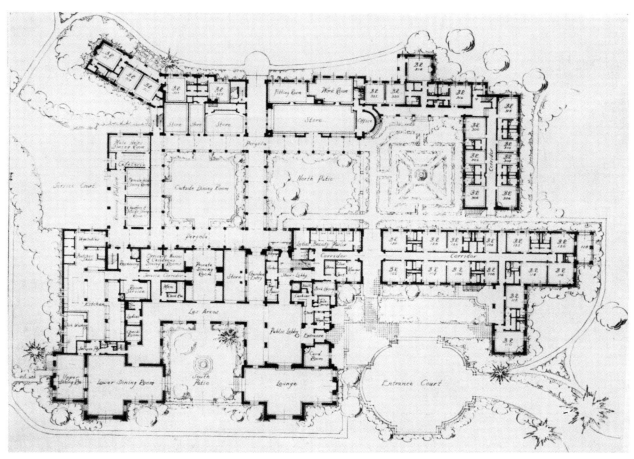

Plan

(*Keystone Photos.*)

Biltmore Hotel, Santa Barbara, California. Reginald D. Johnson, Architect

Plate *118*

Dining Room

Details of Facade　　Biltmore Hotel, Santa Bárbara, California. Reginald D. Johnson, Architect

(Keystone photos)

Plate 119

Hotel

Casino

Golf and Country Club

Agua Caliente Hotel in Mexico, near San Diego, California. Wayne D. McAllister, Architect.

Plate 120

Agua Calienta Spa, Entrance

Hotel Annex

Agua Caliente Hotel in Mexico, near San Diego, California. Wayne D. McAllister, Architect

Plate 121

Agua Caliente Hotel in Mexico, near San Diego, California. Wayne D. McAllister, Architect. — Plunge

Plate 122

Cactus Garden

General View
Hotel El Mirador, Palm Springs, California. Walker and Eisen, Architects

Plate 123

(*Photos. by "Dick" Whittington*)

Tower

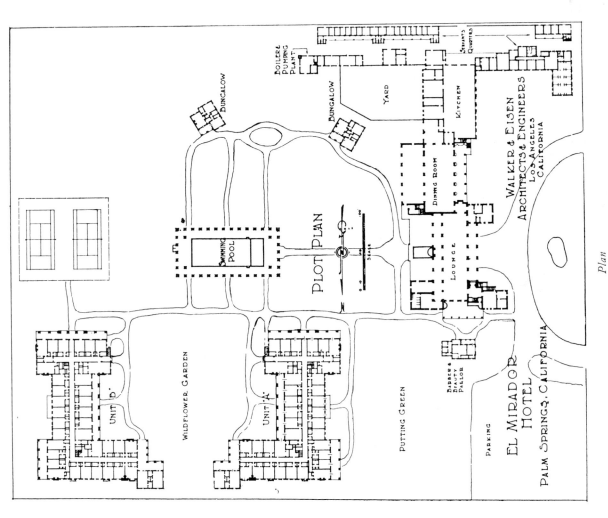

Plan   Hotel El Mirador, Palm Springs, California. Walker and Eisen, Architects

Plate 124

Terrace and Staircase

Lounge Wing

Ojai Valley Country Club, Ojai, California. Wallace Neff, Architect

Plate 125

Lounge

Dining Room   *(Photos by Martin)*

Ojai Country Club, Ojai, California. Wallace Neff, Architect

Plate 126

Little Town Club, Santa Bárbara, California
George Washington Smith, Architect

Daily News Building, Santa Bárbara, California
George Washington Smith, Architect

Plate 127

Lobero Theatre, Santa Bárbara, California. Restoration by George Washington Smith, Architect

Business Premises, Spanish Street, Santa Bárbara, California   (*Photos. by F. G. Anderson*)

Plate 128

Business Premises, Santa Bárbara, California

Business Street, Santa Bárbara, California
(Photos. by F. G. Anderson)

Plate 129

A Richfield Oil Company Service Station, Los Ángeles, California

(Photos. by Mott's Studios)

California House Adapting Excellently the Character and Spirit of California Spanish-Colonial Architecture

Plate 130

Garden Facade

(Photo. by George D. Haigue)

Terrace

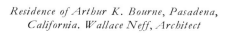

Residence of Arthur K. Bourne, Pasadena,
California. Wallace Neff, Architect

Stair Detail

105198   76325- 120   32C
SPANISH COLONIAL ARCHITECTURE IN THE US
TX6859 910115   02 06-00-00
    LIST PRICE $12.95   NEWCOMB
EVERYDAY PRICE $12.30   0486262634 YN
MEMBERS PRICE $11.07   01/15/91 0110